MASTERWORKS OF JAPANESE ART

MASTERWORKS OF

JAPANESE ART

compiled and edited by
Charles S. Terry

based on the definitive six-volume
Pageant of Japanese Art
edited by staff members of
the Tokyo National Museum

CHARLES E. TUTTLE COMPANY
Rutland, Vermont & Tokyo, Japan

Published by the Charles E. Tuttle Company
of Rutland, Vermont & Tokyo, Japan
with editorial offices at
15 Edogawa-cho, Bunkyo-ku,
Tokyo, Japan

Published by arrangement and in cooperation
with the Toto Bunka-sha of Tokyo,
publishers of the "Pageant of Japanese Art"

Library of Congress Catalog Card No. 56–11126
First edition, July, 1956
Seventh printing, 1960

Printed in Japan

FOREWORD

The Tôto Bunka Company's beautiful *Pageant of Japanese Art* in six volumes is certainly one of the most outstanding Japanese publications since the end of the war. A translation of the same company's *Nihon Bijitsu Zenshu,* it contained some of the most beautiful plates ever made, together with a six-hundred page historical account prepared by a group of the most eminent Japanese scholars in the field. The wide acclaim this publication received created a demand for a more handy volume that would make the excellent work it contained available to a still wider public. Also, since the authoritative original text was compiled for a Japanese audience, it was felt that a general review of it, prepared with an eye toward making it more accessible and comprehensible to readers less versed in Japanese culture would be of great advantage.

In the present volume, therefore, I have tried to extract the essentials from the *Pageant* and present them as simply as the subject permits, with revisions and bits of supplementary information where necessary in the interests of English readers. It is entirely possible that the original editors hold somewhat different ideas as to what the "essentials" are, and they are consequently in no way responsible for the ensuing account. At the same time I should like to express my gratitude for the wealth of data provided me by their work.

In selecting plates from the *Pageant,* I have attempted to choose those that best illustrate the basic historical trends and aesthetic principles, but I was faced with an *embarras de richesses.* It was difficult to part with many of the original reproductions, but I am at least consoled by the fact that those included amply demonstrate the scope and depth of Japan's artistic achievement.

I beg the specialist's indulgence for having attempted to cover such a large subject in so little space. In skipping so lightly over the centuries, I have had to omit much that is important and interesting. Still, if this outline helps to introduce the fascinating subject of Japanese art to the many who are still strangers to it, it will have served a worthy purpose.

CHARLES S. TERRY

CONTENTS

FOREWORD   v

TABLE OF CONTENTS   vii

LIST OF PLATES   viii

LIST OF ILLUSTRATIONS   xi

PART ONE: A SURVEY OF JAPANESE ART

    I   THE PREHISTORIC PERIOD   3

    II   THE ASUKA PERIOD   6

    III THE NARA PERIOD   9

    IV   THE HEIAN PERIOD   16

    V   THE KAMAKURA PERIOD   27

    VI   THE MUROMACHI PERIOD   31

    VII THE MOMOYAMA PERIOD   36

    VIII THE EDO PERIOD   39

    IX   CONCLUSION   45

PART TWO: PLATES

    PAINTING   48

    SCULPTURE   134

    CERAMICS   174

    TEXTILES   194

    LACQUER WARE   204

    METALWORK   210

    ARCHITECTURE   214

INDEX   249

PLATES

PAINTING

* 1   WALL PAINTING *(detail). Nara period.*
* 2   SCREEN PORTRAIT OF A WOMAN *(detail). Nara period.*
* 3   KICHIJÔ-TEN *(detail). Nara period.*
  4   IMAGE OF FUDÔ MYÔ-Ô *(detail). Heian period.*
  5   IMAGE OF KUJAKU MYÔ-Ô. *Heian period.*
* 6   IMAGE OF THE BODHISATTVA FUGEN. *Heian period.*
  7   THE TALE OF GENJI *(detail from the section entitled "Azuma-ya"). Heian period.*
  8   PAINTING ON A SUTRA SCROLL *(detail). Heian period.*
  9   THE HISTORY OF MT. SHIGI *(detail). Heian period.*
 10   FROLIC OF THE ANIMALS *(detail). Heian period.*
 11   FROLIC OF THE ANIMALS *(detail). Heian period.*
 12   HANDBOOK ON ILLNESSES *(detail). Kamakura period.*
*13   THE STORY OF TOMO NO DAINAGON *(detail). Kamakura period.*
 14   ILLUSTRATED *PILLOW BOOK* OF SEI SHÔNAGON *(detail). Kamakura period.*
*15   THE STORY OF THE LATTER THREE YEARS' CAMPAIGN *(detail). Kamakura period.*
 16   PORTRAIT OF MINAMOTO NO YORITOMO *(detail). Kamakura period.*
*17   KÔBÔ DAISHI AS A BOY *(detail). Kamakura period.*
*18   THE THIRTY-SIX IMMORTAL POETS *(section showing Ko Ôgimi). Kamakura period.*
 19   HAN-SHAN, *by Ka-ô (fourteenth century).*
 20   MAN CATCHING A CATFISH WITH A GOURD, *by Josetsu (early fifteenth century).*
 21   WINTER LANDSCAPE, *by Sesshû (1420–1506).*
 22   *HABOKU* LANDSCAPE, *by Sesshû (1420–1506).*
 23   CHOU MAO-SHU VIEWING THE LOTUS FLOWERS, *by Kanô Masanobu (1434–1530).*
 24   STORM AT SEA, *by Sesson (1504–1589?).*
*25   MAPLE-VIEWERS AT MT. TAKAO, *by Kanô Hideyori (middle of the sixteenth century).*
*26   CELEBRATION UNDER THE CHERRY BLOSSOMS *(detail), by Kanô Naganobu (1577–1654).*

[Note] Plates marked with an asterisk (*) are color plates.

27 PLUM TREE, *by Kanô Eitoku (1543-1590)*.

28 PINE TREES, *by Hasegawa Tôhaku (1539-1610)*.

29 SHRIKE ON A DEAD BRANCH, *by Miyamoto Musashi (1584-1645)*.

*30 MIOTSUKUSHI, *by Tawaraya Sôtatsu (early seventeenth century)*.

*31 WESTERNERS PLAYING MUSIC. *Artist unknown. Early seventeenth century.*

32 THE FOUR ACCOMPLISHMENTS, *by Kanô Tan'yû (1602-1674)*.

*33 IRISES, *by Ogata Kôrin (1658-1716)*.

*34 SUMMER AND AUTUMN PLANTS, *by Sakai Hôitsu (1761-1828)*.

*35 CONVENIENCE OF FARMING, *by Ike no Taiga (1723-1776)*.

36 A SUNNY MORNING AT UJI, *by Aoki Mokubei (1775-1833)*.

*37 WOMAN, *by Hishikawa Moronobu (1618-1694)*.

*38 WOMAN ON A VERANDA, *by Suzuki Harunobu (1725-1770)*.

*39 THE FICKLE TYPE, *by Kitagawa Utamaro (1753-1806)*.

40 THE ACTOR BANDÔ MITSUGORÔ, *by Tôshûsai Sharaku (active 1794-95)*.

*41 THE RED FUJI, *by Katsushika Hokusai (1760-1849)*.

*42 BEAUTY *(detail), by Katsushika Hokusai (1760-1849)*.

43 KAMBARA, *by Andô Hiroshige (1797-1858)*.

SCULPTURE

44 *HANIWA* HEAD OF A GIRL. *Prehistoric period.*

45 SHAKA NYORAI. *Asuka period.*

46 KANNON BOSATSU. *Asuka period.*

47 KUDARA KANNON. *Asuka period.*

48 MIROKU BOSATSU. *Asuka period.*

49 KANNON BOSATSU. *Nara period.*

50 BUDDHA HEAD. *Nara period.*

51 AMIDA AND TWO ATTENDANTS. *Nara period.*

52 FUKÛ KENSAKU KANNON. *Nara period.*

53 GAKKÔ BUTSU. *Nara period.*

54 SHÛKONGÔ-JIN. *Nara period.*

55 KÔMOKU-TEN. *Nara period.*

56 THE PRIEST GANJIN. *Nara period.*

57 YAKUSHI NYORAI. *Heian period.*

*58 THE GODDESS NAKATSU-HIME. *Heian period.*

59 AMIDA NYORAI, *by Jôchô (d. 1057)*.

*60 KICHIJÔ-TEN. *Heian period.*

61 MUCHAKU, *by Unkei (late twelfth century)*.

62 TENTÔ-KI, *by Kôben (early thirteenth century)*.

63 BASU SENNIN, *by Tankei (1173-1256)*.

CERAMICS

*64 JÔMON POTTERY. *Prehistoric period.*

*65 JAR: *Three-color glaze. Nara period.*

*66 COVERED DISH: *Oribe pottery. Momoyama period.*

*67 TEA BOWL: *Raku ware, by Hon'ami Kôetsu (1558-1637)*.

*68 VASE: *Iga ware. Edo period.*

*69 VASE: *Kakiemon-type. Edo period.*
*70 DISH: *Imari porcelain. Edo period.*
*71 DISH: *Old Kutani porcelain. Edo period.*
*72 JAR, *by Nonomura Ninsei (seventeenth century).*
*73 BOWL, *by Nin'ami Dôhachi (1783–1855).*

TEXTILES

*74 KANTÔ BROCADE. *Asuka period.*
*75 BROCADE. *Nara period.*
*76 *KOSODE (detail). Edo period.*
*77 NOH COSTUME. *Edo period.*
*78 KIMONO *(detail). Edo period.*

LACQUER WARE

*79 COSMETICS BOX: Maki-e. *Heian period.*
*80 TRAY. *Momoyama period.*
*81 INK-STONE BOX: Maki-e, *by Ogata Kôrin (1658–1716).*

METALWORK

82 KETTLE FOR THE TEA CEREMONY: *Ashiya Type. Muromachi period.*
83 SUTRA BOX. *Muromachi period.*

ARCHITECTURE

84 *HANIWA* HOUSE. *Prehistoric period.*
85 THE MAIN HALL OF THE HÔRYÛ-JI. *Asuka period.*
86 THE FIVE-STORIED PAGODA OF THE HÔRYÛ-JI. *Asuka period.*
87 THE EASTERN PAGODA OF THE YAKUSHI-JI. *Nara period.*
88 THE MAIN HALL OF TÔSHÔDAI-JI. *Nara period.*
89 THE YUME-DONO OF THE HÔRYÛ-JI. *Nara period.*
90 THE PHOENIX HALL OF THE BYÔDÔ-IN. *Heian period.*
91 THE NAGEIRE-DÔ OF THE SAMBUTSU-JI. *Heian period.*
92 THE PAGODA OF THE ISHIYAMA-DERA. *Kamakura period.*
93 THE RELIQUARY HALL OF THE ENGAKU-JI. *Kamakura period.*
94 THE MAIN HALL OF THE KANSHIN-JI. *Muromachi period.*
95 THE SILVER PAVILION. *Muromachi period.*
96 GARDEN OF THE RYÔAN-JI. *Muromachi period.*
97 THE HIMEJI CASTLE. *Momoyama period.*
98 GARDEN AND SHÔKIN-TEI TEAHOUSE OF THE KATSURA PALACE. *Edo period.*
99 VERANDA OF THE SHÔKIN-TEI TEAHOUSE OF THE KATSURA PALACE. *Edo period.*
100 ROOM FOR THE TEA CEREMONY IN THE SHÔKIN-TEI TEAHOUSE. *Edo period,*

ILLUSTRATIONS

1	Clay Figurine. *Jômon period.*	3
2	The Ise Shrine. *The main inner sanctuary and plans for the inner and outer precincts. Pre-Buddhist period.*	4
3	Dôtaku. *Yayoi period.*	5
4	Portrait of Prince Shôtoku and Sons. *Nara period.*	7
5	Painting on the Tamamushi Shrine. *Asuka period.*	8
6	Bronze Nimbus for a Buddhist Statue. *Asuka period.*	9
7 & 8	Hôryû-ji Wall Paintings. *Large panels on the northeast and west walls. Nara period.*	11
9	Entrance to the Main Hall of the Tôshôdai-ji. *Nara period.*	12
10	Landscape on Hemp Cloth (detail). *Nara period.*	14
11	Painting of a Bodhisattva. *Nara period.*	14
12	Tie-Dyed Fabric. *Nara period.*	15
13	Miniature Shingon Pagoda of Early Type. *Heian period.*	17
14	The Diamond Mandala. *Heian period.*	18
15	Chinese Sandalwood Statue. *Sung period.*	19
16	Small Amida Hall and Typical Sanctum.	21
17	Reconstruction of a Nara Palace Building of the Type from which the *Shinden* Style Developed.	22
18	Sections of the *Illustrated Sutra on Cause and Effect. Nara period.*	24
19	*Fukinuke Yatai.*	25
20	Nobleman Clad in Typical Heian Garment.	26
21	Sections from the "Handbook on Hells." *Kamakura period.*	28
22	Portrait of the Priest Kôshô. *Kamakura period.*	29
23	Elevation of the Main Gateway of the Tôdaiji. *Kamakura period.*	30
24	Fabric with Design of Phoenixes and Mallow Blossoms. *Kamakura period.*	30
25	Landscape, by Gaku-ô Zôkyû (late fifteenth century).	32
26	Landscape, by Kanô Motonobu.	33
27	Two Ink-Stone Boxes. *Maki-e. Muromachi period.*	35
28	Maple-Viewers at Mt. Takao, by Kanô Hideyori.	37
29	Ancient Dance, by Sôtatsu.	38
30	Lacquered Container for the Host. *Momoyama period.*	39
31	Tiger, by Kanô Naonobu.	40
32	Sketches from Nature, by Maruyama Ôkyo.	42
33	A Cool Evening, by Torii Kiyonaga .	43
34	Nabeshima Porcelain. *Edo period.*	44
35	Kimono with Yûzen Pattern. *Edo period.*	44

PART ONE A SURVEY OF JAPANESE ART

A SURVEY OF JAPANESE ART

I. THE PREHISTORIC PERIOD
TO A.D. 552

The origins of the Japanese are obscure. In view of strong similarities between the earliest archaeological remains in Japan and specimens that have been excavated in Korea, it seems certain that the first inhabitants came from northern or central Asia. However, the prehistoric culture also contained elements from southern China and, perhaps, Polynesia. No traces of a paleolithic age have been found, but neolithic artifacts dating back to several centuries before Christ have been discovered in quantity.

The earliest inhabitants were a semi-nomadic people who hunted and fished for their sustenance. Though ignorant of the potter's wheel, they made earthern vessels that even today have a strong artistic appeal. These are distinguished by decorative designs suggesting coils of rope, and for this reason they are spoken of as *jômon* ("rope-design") ware, the same term being applied to the culture as a whole. Jômon pottery comes in a wide variety of shapes and sizes. In general, the earlier pieces are purely functional, but even these show a fine sense of form and an understanding of the natural propensities of clay. Many of the later vessels have more or less elaborate decorations, and some are quite pleasing aesthetically. One of the two shown here *(Plate 64 foreground)* has a design that might almost be termed sculptural.

The actual sculpture of this age was limited to clay and was on the whole crude. It falls into two classes: figurines that seem to have had some religious meaning *(Figure 1)*, and simple discs bearing what appear to be human faces. Both types are symmetrical and flat—more pictorial, really, than sculptural—but modern sculptors have been attracted to them because of their simplicity and their mysterious symbolism.

The technique for making lacquer, which had been known in China since very ancient times, seems to have entered Japan in the late Jômon period. Bowls, baskets, bows, arrows, and combs coated with red and black lacquer have been unearthed here and there, the biggest find being a collection from the northern prefecture of Aomori. The pieces are primarily functional, but some of them show a conscious attempt at artistry.

Figure 1. Clay Figurine. Jômon period.

The central section of one black-lacquered bow, for instance, is wrapped with a band of red-lacquered bark, and several of the bowls are black on the outside and red on the inside, like much lacquer ware used in ordinary households today. Unfortunately, these remains cannot be dated, for in some outlying areas the Jômon culture lingered on for centuries after it had disappeared in the central regions.

In the first or second century B. C. a new culture, which also came from the Asiatic continent, began to spread from western Japan. It is known by the name *Yayoi,* since the first samples of its pottery were found at Yayoi-chô in Tokyo. The bearers of the new civilization were the ancestors of the modern Japanese. It is clear that they were an agricultural people, who practiced the wet method of rice cultivation used in southern China. When they arrived they already knew how to cast bronze, and they soon learned also how to forge iron. Metal tools increased their production, and metal weapons gave them a military advantage over the earlier inhabitants, whom they gradually drove back northward or made subjects. Yayoi society was composed of small communities, each organized around a particular clan. As time went on, there emerged great patriarchal families more powerful than the rest. These fought among themselves until eventually the one that occupied the fertile and populous Yamato Plain, near modern Kyoto, succeeded in gaining at least nominal authority over the others. This eventually became the Japanese imperial family, but it should be observed that

the concept of an emperor was a comparatively late innovation from China and not really an integral part of Yayoi culture.

Yayoi pottery is technically better than that of the previous age, but less imaginative. It is plain and conventional in shape, and its surface designs are simple and linear. It appears to have been turned on the wheel by professional potters and produced in comparatively large quantities.

From the third century on, the major clans built huge tumuli for their dead scions, and as a consequence the era that lasted from then until the sixth century is known as the "period of the ancient burial mounds." Around and on top of the great tombs of this age were placed groups of sculptured figures known as *haniwa.* These statues, though primitive in themselves, were a great improvement over the flat figurines of the Jômon culture. They were fully three-dimensional and were made in many shapes and sizes. Some were images of men or women, and others of wild or domestic animals, while a third group represented houses, vehicles, weapons, and other inanimate objects. Each had a cylindrical base (or bases) so that it could be stuck into the ground. The *haniwa* were made by an interesting method called *wazumi* ("piles of rings"), which is exactly what the term suggests: rings of clay were stacked in the general shape desired, the surfaces smoothed, and the statue fired at a low temperature. The resulting images were unsophisticated, but therein lies their charm. They were as simple, as innocent, and as cheerful as the primitive Japanese poetry preserved in the oldest historical texts.

Figure 2. The Ise Shrine. The main inner sanctuary and plans for the inner and outer precincts. Pre-Buddhist period.

There is a clear distinction between the *haniwa* of the central area and those of outlying regions. The former are relatively polished and uniform in style, while the latter tend to be rougher and to vary in style from place to place. This, incidentally, is true of sculpture in the more advanced ages. Despite the stylistic differences, however, all *haniwa* were made in essentially the same fashion. They were hollow, and in the case of those representing humans or animals, the eyes and mouths consisted merely of simple perforations. It is surprising how beautiful some of these figures are. The head shown here *(Plate 44)*, which is typical of the *haniwa* from the central region, captures the artlessness of a very young woman, the softness of her plump cheeks, the wonder in her facial expression. The sculptor who made this statue was already prepared to learn the techniques needed to produce the magnificent Buddhist images of the succeeding period.

It has long been known that in addition to cave dwellings, the early Japanese had pit houses, ground-level houses, and raised-floor houses. Until recently, it was generally supposed that the superstructures of these buildings consisted of simple gabled roofs, such as those of the Ise Shrine *(Figure 2)*, which is the most archaic building actually in existence. (As a matter of fact, the shrine has been reconstructed fifty-eight times, but every effort has been made to avoid change, and to judge from descriptions in early manuscripts, it does not seem to differ greatly from its original form.) It has now been shown, however, that the arrangement of pillars most often observed in the sites of early pit houses would not allow for the construction of such a roof, and it appears that the outward-leaning gables and rounded ridges of the *haniwa* house shown here *(Plate 84)* were the more usual. Many of the simpler dwellings seem to have been in the form of a truncated cone with a roof of this type added almost as an afterthought. Of course, this was not actually the case, but these bulky, outswept roofs do suggest architectural considerations over and above the practical need for a covering. Unfortunately, the buildings of this era cannot be studied thoroughly, since they were made of wood and thatch and have consequently long since perished.

Having succeeded in unifying the Japanese, the Yamato clan undertook to annex the Korean peninsula. They were in the long run unsuccessful, but for two or three centuries they managed to maintain a colony in southern Korea. The effect of this on Asian politics was as nothing compared with its influence on the culture of Japan. Even in the period of which we are speaking, much of the material culture of China was adopted. Most important, perhaps, were metal objects—the swords, shields, helmets, and horse trappings that constituted military strength. It might be noted that even the implements of war from this early age are frequently too elaborate in design to have been made by any but the most expert craftsmen, and mirrors, along with the bell-like objects called *dôtaku (Figure 3)*, show even more skill.

The mirrors were copied from Chinese models, but the *dôtaku* are unique to Japan. No one knows quite what they were used for. Most of them have no clappers, but they could have been and at first probably were rung with mallets. In later times they were not actually used, but were regarded as treasures of some sort, perhaps even as objects of

Figure 3. Dôtaku. *Yayoi period.*

art. Some of them are decorated with geometric designs, whereas others have scenes from everyday life cast on them in relief. These drawings were simply executed, but they reveal many facts about prehistoric Japanese civilization, and they are about the only source of information that we have on Japanese painting of this era. Presumably there *was* painting, and it was probably somewhat less crude than the pictures cast in bronze, but no actual specimens have survived.

During this period Yayoi pottery continued to develop, but it was eventually superseded by a superior type imported from Silla, a contemporary kingdom in southern Korea. The new pottery, which was shaped on the wheel and baked at a high temperature, was both beautiful and strong.

The color was usually grayish, and on some pieces there are drops of a beautiful natural glaze. Wares of this type were produced in large numbers, and they tend toward uniformity of shape, but there are several noteworthy exceptions. By this time artists and craftsmen had been organized into hereditary guilds according to their specialty. Most of these centered at first around foreign craftsmen who had for one reason or another immigrated to Japan, but as time went on, there was less need for teachers from abroad.

To summarize, all the major crafts advanced to a high level of achievement during the period of the ancient burial mounds, but painting, sculpture and architecture had to await the inspiration that Buddhism was to provide.

II. THE ASUKA PERIOD
552 — 645

Buddhism was long thought to have been officially introduced to Japan in 552, but contemporary scholars accept the year 538 as the most accurate date. At that time King Syöng-myöng of Pekché, on the Korean peninsula, presented to the Japanese Emperor Kimmei (reigned 532?–570) a gold-covered bronze statue of Sakyamuni Buddha, together with sutra scrolls and decorative Buddhist banners. Prior to this there had been a few Buddhist immigrants, but the rulers had shown no sign of interest in the foreign religion. Now, however, the imperial family and some of its supporters began to concern themselves more and more with the importation of the faith and of the continental culture centered about it. The propagation of the new religion was not so simple as it has frequently been made to sound in later accounts. As is usual in such instances, it became ensnared in politics. The Soga clan, who had not previously been very important, became its outspoken champions, probably detecting in it a means of gaining power. On the other hand, the Mononobe, who were the traditional warriors of the state, recognized it as a threat to their political security and tried in various ways to suppress it. After several ups and downs the Buddhists, or perhaps we should simply say the Soga, won. Because of the conflict between these two groups

the first Buddhist temple in Japan was not constructed until 588. In the meantime, Buddhist art, sculpture in particular, seems to have been imported in fair quantity. According to the earliest official history, the *Chronicles of Japan (Nihon Shoki)*, Buddhist statues arrived from the Korean state of Koguryö in 562; sculptors and architects came from Pekché in 577; more statues were presented by the third Korean state, Silla, in 579; and a stone statue of Maitreya was sent by Pekché in 584. During the five-year reign of the Emperor Sushun (588–592) it is recorded that architects, tilemakers, a metalworker, and a painter arrived from Pekché. Meanwhile, in 587, a new epoch began when a sculptor named Kuratsukuribe no Tasuna, who was born in Japan, made a Buddhist image sixteen feet high in memory of the Emperor Yômei (reigned 585–586).

In 593 the Empress Suiko came to the throne with her able nephew Prince Shôtoku (574–622) as regent *(Figure 4)*. The latter may be regarded as the real founder of Japanese Buddhism. Aside from being well acquainted with the scriptures, he was extremely active in promoting the spread of the faith. When he came to power only two or three temples existed, but in 624, two years after his death, there were forty-six monasteries and nunneries, 816 priests, and 569 nuns. The prince is credited variously with having had from seven to all of the religious centers constructed. Of them, the most important for our purposes is the Hôryû-ji, erected by Shôtoku and Suiko in memory of the Emperor Yômei. When completed in 607, this temple was filled with Chinese-style icons and other works of art, many of which survive today. According to certain documentary evidence, the buildings themselves burned in 670, but many art critics maintain that this is not so, and, in any event, the main hall *(Plate 85)*, pagoda *(Plate 86)*, inner gate, and surrounding corridors appear to have retained their original Asuka form until the present. They are the oldest wooden buildings in the world.

Of the many art objects in the Hôryû-ji, one of the most important historically is the central icon in the main hall, a bronze image of Sakyamuni Buddha *(Plate 45)* flanked by two attendants. An inscription on the back of this statue says that it was made in the thirty-first year of the reign of Suiko (623) by the sculptor Tori and dedicated to the peaceful afterlife of Prince Shôtoku, who had died the previous year. This Tori was the son of Kuratsukuribe no Tasuna, mentioned above, and the grandson of one of the first Buddhists in Japan, a man of Chinese stock named Shiba Tachito. These three men all worked energetically to propagate the Buddhist faith, and they accordingly enjoyed the patronage of emperors who were converted to it. Tori is said to have been a great favorite of Prince Shôtoku and to have been awarded a high rank along with a large area of rice fields for his services. We mention these details not only because this is the first instance of an artist attaining such prominence, but also because Tori's was one of the two main styles of the Asuka period. The Sakyamuni in the Hôryû-ji is the only image that can be definitely attributed to him, but there are several contemporary works that might well be either by him or by one of his followers. The Yume-dono Kannon *(Plate 46)*, for example, is in almost the same style as the Sakyamuni triad, although the subject is so different that this is not at first obvious. Both statues were intended to be seen from the front and are consequently quite flat. Far from being realistic, they are symmetrical and conventionalized. The proportions of the bodily parts are unnatural, the heads and limbs in the triad being disproportionately large,

Figure 4. Portrait of Prince Shôtoku and Sons. Nara period.

and the entire body of the Kannon being exaggeratedly tall and thin. In shape, the individual images have been made to approximate isosceles triangles, so that they seem exceptionally stable. Although the faces are longer than those of Nara period icons, the cheeks are relatively full. The eyes are wide open, in contrast with the half-shut eyes of later eras, while the mouths are crescents with slightly upturned ends, suggestive of the "archaic smile" found in early Greek sculpture. In general, the facial features are large. The ears are long and flat, which is usual, but they lack the perforations in the lobes found in the Nara and later periods. The fingernails project beyond the fingertips—a characteristic not subsequently found until the Kamakura period, during which the Chinese style of the Sung period (960–1279) came into vogue. The necks are long and cylindrical, and that of Sakyamuni is without the three circular grooves universal in later statues of the Buddhas. Sakyamuni's attendants and the Kannon have these, incised in fine lines, but as a rule they were omitted in Asuka images. One might itemize a large number of less prominent features, such as details in clothing and in mounting, but it will suffice here to say by way of summary that the Tori style emphasized the front view and sacrificed realism for decorative effect. On the whole, this type of sculpture derives from that of the latter part of the Chinese Northern Wei period (386–534). It should be noted that there was a time lag of something like a century before the style reached Japan.

During the same era, we find statues of a slightly different type that appear to have originated in a style prevalent in China around the end of the sixth century and the beginning of the seventh. The most celebrated example is the Kudara Kannon *(Plate 47)*, which is classed with the Yume-dono Kannon as one of the two great masterpieces of wooden sculpture from the Asuka period. In over-all form, the Kudara Kannon is much the same as statues in the Tori style, but the treatment is more three-dimensional, and the bodily proportions appear somewhat more natural. The scarf-ends, instead of spreading out flatly as in the case of the Yume-dono Kannon, curl up forward, thus adding depth. The surface is thickly coated with priming for color, so that the statue appears softer and warmer than the Yume-dono image, which is in effect a plain wooden version of a bronze statue.

The development from the Yume-dono Kannon to the Kudara Kannon did not take place in Japan. The two statues represent Chinese styles which were originally a hundred years or so apart, but which were brought to Japan at about the same time. This, however, is not to say that there was no stylistic development in Japan during the period in question. By the late years of the Asuka period, both the Tori style and that of the Kudara Kannon changed conspicuously, particularly the latter, which became the form typified by the justly renowned Maitreya in the Chûgû-ji *(Plate 48)*.

In addition to statues, many other relics of the Asuka period are preserved in the Hôryû-ji. The most instructive perhaps is the famous Tamamushi Shrine, the name of which derives from the fact that it is decorated with the beautiful wings of an insect known as the *tamamushi (chrysochroa elegans)*. The shrine consists of a miniature palace hall (with hipped and gabled roof) set on a high pedestal. The outside surface is decorated with pictures in red, yellow, and green lacquer on a black lacquer background. Of particular interest are two paintings on the pedestal which depict experiences of the Buddha during his early incarnations *(Figure 5)*. Both stories are told through a series of events depicted on the same surface—a technique that might be regarded as precursive to the mode of expression in Japanese scroll paintings. The only other item indicative of the nature of Asuka painting is an embroidered cloth, owned by the Chûgû-ji and dating from 622. This was originally a large tapestry showing a panoramic view of the Buddhist paradise, but only small fragments have been preserved. Documentation of the work, however, is unusually complete, and we know even the names of the persons who drew the underpaintings for the embroidered designs.

The Hôryû-ji collection contains numerous other samples of textiles from this period, including brocades as well as simpler fabrics. One of the most interesting specimens is the "Kantô Brocade," a handsome piece of red material supposed to

Figure 5. Painting on the Tamamushi Shrine. Asuka period.

have been used as a decorative banner on an occasion when Prince Shôtoku lectured on the scriptures *(Plate 74)*. The cloth is really not a brocade, but a *kasuri* weave; that is to say, it was woven of threads that had first been dyed in segments so as to produce the desired decorative pattern. *Kasuri* is unknown among the early fabrics of China and Korea, and its appearance in Japan during this age is surprising. The technique by which it was made is similar to one common today in the South Sea Islands, however, and it is possible that this fabric came directly or indirectly from that region.

Practically no samples of ceramic ware from the Asuka period remain, and one can only conjecture that the pottery of the previous period, which was of superior quality, continued to be produced. Metalwork, already at a high level at the beginning of the period, became even more refined. Witness the amazingly delicate openwork in the bronze nimbus shown here, which is only twenty centimeters high *(Figure 6)*. The perforated metal crown of the Yume-dono Kannon *(Plate 46)* is another fine illustration of the same technique.

The aesthetic development of the Asuka period remains to a considerable extent a matter of guess, since most of the works from that age long

Figure 6. Bronze Nimbus for a Buddhist Statue. Asuka period.

ago disappeared. Students of Japanese art can hardly complain, however, since they have in the Hôryû-ji and its possessions a source of information unmatched anywhere in the world for that period.

III. THE NARA PERIOD
6 4 5 — 7 9 4

One of the most important changes that occurred under the enlightened leadership of Prince Shôtoku was the establishment of direct contact with China. Before, Japan had always carried on intercourse through the intermediation of one of the states on the Korean peninsula, but in 607 a mission was sent to the Sui court and thereafter a long series of Japanese travelers had the privilege of seeing continental civilization at first hand. In China the Sui (590–618) soon gave way to the T'ang (618–906), but the foundation had been laid for a glorious new epoch. The cultural energy of the Chinese now exploded with a force that was felt throughout the civilized world. Traditional Chinese arts and letters reached unprecedented heights, and they were further enriched by im-

portations from India, Persia, Arabia, and the other Western regions. During its most flourishing years T'ang China forged what might be termed a "world culture," and this made a profound impression on the Japanese, who proceeded to try to make it their own. For more than two centuries after Shôtoku's first embassy, officials, priests, and students were sent to China to learn about government, religion, literature, and the arts. Within Japan something on the order of a revolution, later known as the Taika Reform, occurred in 645, when the Japanese rulers, wisely or unwisely, tried to establish Chinese political and social principles in their kingdom. Chinese ideas of government, it may be observed, were largely incompatible with actual economic conditions in

Japan, and the practical results of the reform were questionable from the first. Nevertheless, a new ideal for the nation had been given official approval, and no matter how remote it was from reality, it dominated the thinking of the time. During the succeeding two hundred years the main business of Japan was the wholesale adoption of Chinese civilization, and this is particularly obvious in contemporary art. It must be noted, however, that, while the artists of the era were at first closely bound to Chinese precedents, they soon began to depart, or at least to digress, from them. By the middle of the eighth century, they had created truly native forms of expression, particularly in the field of sculpture. The statuary of this epoch represents in fact a pinnacle of Japanese aesthetic attainment.

Buddhism, which under the rule of the Empress Suiko and Prince Shōtoku had played a large part in government, appears to have suffered a setback in the course of the semi-Confucianist Taika Reform, but it soon recaptured its pivotal position, apparently as a result of the strong personal faith of several consecutive emperors. During the latter part of the seventh century, the court was able, with the aid of a few powerful clans, to extend its authority over many of the unruly provincial nobles, and there gradually developed a centralized government with at least a formal resemblance to the ideal envisioned by the Taika reformers.

Before close relations with China were established, the Japanese had habitually transferred the seat of government upon the succession of each new emperor. Now, however, the population was steadily increasing, a Chinese-style bureaucracy was taking shape, and large permanent monasteries were being built, so that it was becoming exceedingly inconvenient and expensive to move the capital every few years. In the course of time, therefore, several plans were devised for the erection of a fixed capital city modeled on that of the T'ang at Ch'ang-an, and in the late seventh century such a city took form at Fujiwara, in the Asuka district, south of present-day Nara. Aside from palaces and houses, great monasteries were built in that locality with ever-increasing rapidity, and it is recorded that by 681 there were twenty-four in all. Architecturally the most outstanding were the Daikan-daiji and the Yakushi-ji, the former because of its great size, and the latter

because of its unusual building arrangement. Not a single hall of the Daikan-daiji stands today, but the surviving portions of the foundation show that the buildings were laid out according to the Hōryū-ji system and that the base of the pagoda was fifty-four feet square. The latter seems to have been a nine-storied tower, probably the largest built in Japan up to that time.

The Yakushi-ji was erected by the Emperor Temmu (673–686) in the superstitious hope of securing his consort's recovery from an eye disease. The buildings were largely completed by 689, and even though the monastery was moved to Nara only a few years later, they are said to have retained their original form. Among them, only the Eastern Pagoda (Plate 87) is still standing. Excellent artistically, it is also invaluable as the one existing sample of architecture from the early Nara period. The plan of the Yakushi-ji as a whole was transitional. It called for two pagodas, as was usual in later times, but they were enclosed within the surrounding corridors in the Hōryū-ji manner.

A remarkable bronze statue from this age is housed in one of the halls of the modern Yakushi-ji. An image of Kannon (Plate 49), it shows the strong influence of T'ang art and indirectly of Gupta art, but it has an air of gentleness and serenity not found in its continental prototypes. Contemporary with this work are the head of a Buddha found in the Kōfuku-ji some years ago (Plate 50) and the small triad housed in Lady Tachibana's Shrine (Plate 51). This last is very characteristic of the transition from the Asuka style to that of the mature Nara period. The treatment in general is more naturalistic than in Asuka sculpture, the faces being fatter, the eyes longer and narrower, and the general contours less angular. The attendants stand with their bodies slightly bent at the waist instead of rigidly erect, and the clothing, which is of the type known in Indian art as "wet drapery," falls in easy folds and curves rather than in stylized patterns. On the other hand, there remain certain features of the Asuka period, such as the crescent mouths, the flat unpierced ear lobes, and the absence of the usual lines on the neck.

It is worth mentioning here that the outside of Lady Tachibana's Shrine is decorated with pictures of various Buddhist beings painted in gold paste on a lacquered base. These are not

Figures 7 & 8. Hôryû-ji Wall Paintings. Large panels on the northeast and west walls. Nara period.

nearly as famous or important as the contemporary wall paintings in the main hall of the Hôryû-ji *(Plate 1 and Figures 7 & 8)*, which they resemble in style, but since the latter have been virtually destroyed, they have become the only actual relics of Buddhist painting in the early Nara period. Both sets of paintings reflect the same strong influence of the T'ang that was mentioned in the case of Nara statues, and the wall paintings, at least, had features that were quite Indian. Specifically, the figures in them were drawn with pronounced three-dimensional effect, and the contours were of the thin, unvarying type known as "iron-wire" lines. In general, the murals were executed in much the same style as the cave pictures at Ajanta. However, it would be a mistake to conclude that they represented a case of direct Indian influence. The Indian methods must simply have been among the many foreign elements absorbed into T'ang art and later transmitted to Japan.

From the first it was felt by many that the Fujiwara capital was too far south, and, in any event, the topography of the area was deemed by astrologers unsuitable for the chief city of the realm. Consequently, in 710 the Empress Gemmyô, with the idea of founding, once and for all, a permanent seat of government, transferred her

palace and administration northward to Nara. There a metropolis was erected on virtually the same plan and scale as Ch'ang-an. This was an extravagance, no doubt, but one that must have given the early Japanese the pleasant feeling that they had at last arrived—that they now had a capital befitting the dignity of a modern civilized nation. The important monasteries in the Fujiwara district followed the court to Nara, where they set about building new and usually larger quarters. The government sponsored most of the construction projects, and even in cases when this was not so, the tax-free monasteries had so much land and wealth that the new temples were often as magnificent as those gracing the T'ang capital. Not much is known of the secular buildings in Nara, which have long since burned or collapsed, but a number of the Buddhist structures are still in relatively good condition.

The spread of Buddhism and of Buddhist architecture was no longer limited to the urban area, as it had inclined to be in the past. In 741 the Emperor Shômu issued an edict ordering that a monastery and a convent be built in every province, and while this command was not carried out to the letter, it sufficed to introduce Buddhism and Buddhist art to many outlying districts. In

745, Shômu officially announced a plan to erect a huge bronze statue of the Buddha, into which were to be poured "all the copper resources in the country," and a hall to house this colossus to be built by "reclaiming a great mountain." The ruler's intention was to found a central monastery that would serve as the hub of the system formed by the provincial monasteries and convents. He sought to propagate the Buddhist faith throughout the land, and thereby to secure the Buddha's blessing for the nation. At the same time, he could not have been entirely blind to the prestige that both he and his country would gain by erecting this gigantic monument.

An early record says that 50,000 woodworkers, 370,000 metalworkers, and 2,180,000 laborers were engaged in the construction of the monastery, which is known as the Tôdaiji. It is also recorded that the statue of the Great Buddha, approximately fifty-eight feet high, was completed only after an eight-part casting requiring three years, and that 451,000 catties of copper, 21,000 catties of gold, and 100 catties of tin went into it. The hall housing it was about 290 feet wide, 170 feet deep, and 156 feet high. Directly to the north at some distance was a large lecture hall, while to the

south were the inner gateway and main southern gateway. In the space between the latter on the east and west sides there were two seven-storied pagodas, each over three hundred feet high. Behind the lecture hall lay dormitories for priests, libraries, and numerous other buildings. In addition there were connecting or surrounding corridors totaling 154 "bays" in length, a "bay" being the distance between columns, usually around nine feet.

Unfortunately, the Tôdaiji was largely destroyed by fire in 1180 and again in 1567. The Great Buddha still stands, but it has undergone countless repairs, and from the first it seems to have been more imposing than beautiful. The only important architectural remain of the original monastery is a part of a small temple named the Hokke-dô, which incidentally was the first of the buildings completed, but the brief account given above indicates several general truths about Buddhist architecture in the Nara period. First, it was often on a scale that would be prohibitive even today, especially if the material were wood. Second, it emphasized symmetry in plan, to the extent that the larger monasteries would have been out of place, if not impossible to build, anywhere except

Figure 9. Entrance to the Main Hall of the Tôshôdai-ji. Nara period.

on relatively level ground. Finally, it enjoyed the financial support of the rulers.

The principal sanctuaries of the great official monasteries, which were the most outstanding architectural achievements of the period, were all built of wood, and not one has withstood the ravages of time. The most important structure of this type still standing is the main hall of the Tôshôdai-ji *(Plate 88 and Figure 9)*, a monastery founded by the renowned Chinese missionary Chien-chên (688–763), or, as he is known in Japan, Ganjin, who transmitted the monastic discipline to Japan. The plan for the Tôshôdai-ji is said to have been drawn up in 759, and this hall is considered to date from some time between then and the end of the Nara period. Ganjin enjoyed the support of the court and the common people alike, and as a result he was able to construct buildings nearly as large in scale as the official temples. Moreover, they were built at a time when the architectural techniques of the Nara epoch had reached full maturity. The main hall is, accordingly, a superb building executed in a massive, forceful style. It teaches us a great deal about the form and design of the larger Nara period edifices.

The Hôryû-ji has been discussed as an example of Asuka architecture, but we should not overlook that it also contains fine buildings from the Nara epoch. We have included here the Yume-dono *(Plate 89)*, which houses the statue of Kannon in the style of Tori mentioned above *(Plate 46)*. This octagonal hall unfortunately underwent several changes while being repaired in the Kamakura period, but it is still the finest building of its sort in Japan, and it serves as an illustration of the smaller structures in Nara monasteries.

The late Nara period witnessed the creation of some of the most beautiful Buddhist statues ever made and is for this reason usually considered the golden age of Japanese sculpture. Previously, sculptors had worked almost exclusively in bronze, but now they began also to use clay, lacquer, and, to a lesser degree, stone. The main stylistic developments can immediately be seen by comparing the Fukû Kensaku Kannon *(Plate 52)* in the Hokke-dô with the Shô Kannon *(Plate 49)* in the Yakushi-ji. The later statue, one observes, is more realistic, better proportioned, and heavier in face and body. It is clearly related to the strong, solid style of the mature T'ang, and Indian elements, though

present, are less pronounced than in the earlier work. To be sure, the image has six arms and three eyes like the Hindu Siva, but nevertheless it has none of the lithe, somewhat careless attitude of Indian deities, whereas the older statue does. We might point out in passing that the silver crown on the Fukû Kensaku Kannon is one of the most highly admired pieces of metalwork from this period.

Flanking the Fukû Kensaku Kannon are two smaller clay statues representing the Buddhas of the sun and the moon. Their basic lines are also Chinese, but the faces and the general softness of treatment are Japanese. These deities must originally have been extremely colorful, for there are remnants of gold leaf on their hair and of green and cinnabar on their clothing. Shown here is the Buddha of the moon *(Plate 53)*, which is in better condition than its companion piece.

Although statues of fierce aspect were not as common in the Nara period as later, quite a number of them were made. The clay image of Shûkongô-jin (Vajrapani) now situated back to back with the Fukû Kensaku Kannon is a good example *(Plate 54)*. According to a collection of Buddhist legends edited early in the Heian period, the monk Rôben, prior to founding the Tôdaiji, lived in a small temple on the site where the Hokke-dô was later built and daily worshiped before this statue. If this story is true, this work is older than the Kannon and the other statues in the same building. As a matter of fact, it does have a somewhat antique air about it, but in general style it is much the same as the Four Deva Kings in the Tôdaiji Hall of Ordination *(Plate 55)*, which, along with the Buddhas of the sun and moon, represent the culmination of Nara clay sculpture. The Deva Kings are in more subdued poses than the Shûkongô-jin, but all were modeled with the same techniques, and all have the same muscular, lifelike bodies.

A certain urge toward realism evident in the Buddhist sculpture already mentioned found a more satisfactory outlet in portraits of priests, which were not circumscribed by canonical rules. An excellent example, and indeed one of the most moving works in all Japanese art, is the statue of the blind and ancient Ganjin shown here *(Plate 56)*. This image, like the Fukû Kensaku Kannon, was made by the dry-lacquer method described below, which allowed for very free modeling of details in the facial expression.

In 756 the Emperor Shômu died, and his widow, the Empress Kômyô, presented the Tôdaiji with a large collection of his personal treasures as well as the religious implements that had been employed at the ceremony for "opening the eyes" of the Great Buddha in 752. These articles were placed in the main storehouse of the monastery, known as the Shôsô-in, where many of them have been preserved until today. They include a great variety of art objects from China and other countries as well as from Japan itself. In addition to Buddhist paraphernalia, there are paintings, documents, writing equipment, musical instruments, clothing, eating and drinking utensils, weapons, and numerous other items. Also, there still exists a catalogue of the collection, which bears the date 756, and which provides much information on objects now missing as well as on those still extant. The contents of this unique repository make it possible to study the painting and crafts of the Nara period, of which there are elsewhere very few relics.

Five or six actual paintings have been preserved in the Shôsô-in. Among them are two screen portraits of ladies, one of which is shown here *(Plate 2)*. Originally the woman's clothing was

Figure 11. Painting of a Bodhisattva. Nara period.

adorned with bird feathers, after a current Chinese fashion, but these have come off, and only the underpainting is left. It resembles some early portraits that have been unearthed in Central Asia, but we should not infer that Japan was in direct contact with that region. Instead, it appears that the woman in this painting, with her fat and matronly, but sensuous, face, her brightly painted lips, and her heavily rouged cheeks, was a Chinese ideal that was adopted in outlying countries. A similar painting has been preserved in the Yakushi-ji *(Plate 3)*. Strictly speaking it is an image of the goddess of fortune, Kichijô-ten (Mahasri), whose cult was strong in Nara Japan, but it looks more like a perfectly secular portrait of a great beauty. No doubt, the Japanese of this era sought in the benign goddess, who bestows money, treasures, food, and other material benefits, a vision of the perfect woman. It might be noted that the same conception of Kichijô-ten is to be observed in many later works, such as the famous sculptured image in the Jôruri-ji *(Plate 60)*, which dates from the twelfth century.

Aside from the two screen portraits of women, the most important paintings in the Shôsô-in are a landscape *(Figure 10)* and the image of a Bodhisattva *(Figure 11)*, both executed in ink on hemp cloth. The lines in the former are thin and delicate, while those in the latter are heavy and bold, but despite this difference, both paintings

Figure 10. Landscape on Hemp Cloth (detail). Nara period.

are prototypes of the magnificent ink monochromes produced in China during the Sung period (960–1279) and in Japan somewhat later than that.

According to the list of 756, there were originally one hundred screens in the Shôsô-in, of which twenty-one were decorated with paintings and seventy-five with batik or stencil-dyed pictures. Many of the names imply strictly secular subjects ("Landscape," "Chinese Picture of an Archaic Palace," "Simple Sketch of Evening Revelries," etc.), and although some or all of these may have come from China, it is practically certain that Japanese painters were also called upon to produce works of the same type. Consequently, while a purely native secular art did not develop until later, there is a strong possibility that it had its beginnings in this age.

A hasty glance at the various developments in the crafts during the Nara period shows rapid improvements resulting not only from frequent intercourse with China but also from governmental organization of craftsmen. According to the legal code promulgated in 701, bureaus were established in the various branches of the imperial government to meet palace needs for equipment that had formerly been made by various hereditary guilds. There were a Bureau of Potters, a Bureau of the Palace Wardrobe, an Office of the Guild of Needleworkers, an Office of the Guild of Weavers, a Bureau of Metalworkers, a Bureau of Woodworkers, an Office of the Guild of Lacquer Workers, and so on. In contrast to many of the other Chinese-style administrative offices, these seem to have been quite active.

In the field of ceramics the most important innovation was the adoption of colored glazes. The technique of low-temperature baking employed in the famous T'ang three-color pieces, was apparently introduced by way of Korea or the Po-hai kingdom in the early part of the eighth century. It was soon mastered and used on a variety of wares, samples of which are preserved in the Shôsô-in. There has been considerable discussion as to whether these utensils in the Shôsô-in are of Chinese or Japanese make, but it is now generally agreed that they are Japanese. For one thing, while the patterns are like those on T'ang wares, they lack the variety and freedom of the latter. Also, the raw material, in contrast to the extremely fine clay used in T'ang pieces, is rough and grayish, like that used in Japanese

roof tiles during this period. Finally, although the glazes contain about the same chemical ingredients as those of China, they do not have the same smooth, rich finish. Shown here *(Plate 65)* is a covered vessel excavated near Osaka. Its glaze is like that of some of the Shôsô-in items with which it is roughly contemporaneous, but its shape is unique. It was modeled after a type of metal reliquary that was then in frequent use, but, of course, being made of clay, it is softer in appearance.

According to the land laws of the Nara period, each household was allotted an area for the cultivation of mulberry and lacquer trees. No doubt the demand for silk and lacquer to be used in Buddhist buildings, furnishings, images, and so on was so great that the government had to take official steps to insure a sufficient supply. Techniques for making cloth and lacquer articles improved tremendously. Wood and bamboo had long been used as frames for lacquered objects, but now the dry-lacquer *(kanshitsu)* technique which had been brought from China came into fashion.

This method, which as we have seen was also

Figure 12. Tie-Dyed Fabric. Nara period.

used by sculptors, called for making a wooden frame roughly in the shape desired and covering it with layers of cloth that had been dipped in lacquer. Surface details were modeled before the material dried. Objects made in this way lack the sharp corners and edges of those made with wood, and as a result they frequently seem softer and more appealing. Since, however, the method imposed restrictions on shape and involved a good deal of bother, it was virtually abandoned after the Nara period.

Ways were devised to decorate plain lacquer surfaces with gold, silver, mother-of-pearl, tortoise shell, and other colorful or precious materials. The simplest method, and the most common during the Nara period, was to cut out a design from a thin sheet of gold or silver, apply it to the wet lacquered surface, and later cover it with additional coats of lacquer. Some objects were decorated with inlaid mother-of-pearl, often in combination with gold, silver, or some other substance. Designs were also made with gold paint, with a mixture of gold dust and glue, and with plain gold dust sprinkled on the damp lacquer. Patterns of the last type, known as *maki-e,* eventually became the most popular *(Plate 81).*

Perhaps the greatest advances were made in the field of textiles. Brocades of the most elaborate sort were produced *(Plate 75),* along with beautiful figured silks, tapestries, and an intricate gauzy material called *ra,* in which four warp threads were intertwined in varying arrangements. The last is so complicated that it looks almost like a knitted fabric. It ceased to be made shortly after the Nara period and thereafter until the twentieth century was considered impossible to reproduce. Along with these woven silks, several kinds of dyed fabrics were in use. One of the most interesting was batik, which was made by drawing the pattern in a wax resist and then dipping the cloth in dye. This method, said to have been invented in ancient India, seems to have been fairly common during the Nara period, but is not found in later epochs. Figured fabrics were also made by stencil-dyeing and tie-dyeing, the latter being the oldest and most widely used method of all. Usually pinches of cloth were tied tightly with strings before dipping, and the result was a simple pattern of small white circles *(Figure 12).* Various more complicated tie-dyed materials existed, but the technique, while simple, did not allow a great deal of freedom. Printed figures, as well as embroidery, are found on some Nara fabrics.

IV. THE HEIAN PERIOD

794 — 1185

During the reign of the Emperor Shômu (724–749), the authority of the crown was secure, and the nation was relatively firmly united. The powerful clans, however, had by no means been destroyed, but had simply become members of the national bureaucracy. As such, they were politically strong enough to consolidate their social and economic position, and their subsequent success in so doing spelled the end of imperial control, already weakened by the extravagant support that the government had been giving to the Buddhist religion. The court had not only undertaken to pay for the building of temples, the copying of sutras, and the other activities essential to religious proselytizing, but had also exempted the monasteries from the land tax, a consideration also extended to many of the nobility. In other words,

although the government was in danger of being overthrown by rich noblemen and of depleting its funds on Buddhist projects, it continued to grant tax exemptions to these same noblemen and to Buddhist establishments. This was, of course, economically and politically disastrous.

Some years after the death of Shômu, a priest named Dôkyô won the patronage of the Empress Shôtoku (reigned 764–769) to the extent that she was on the point of abdicating in his favor. A group of nobles, however, finally managed to prevent this by securing a dictum against it from the Sun Goddess. Dôkyô was later discredited, and there followed something of a reaction against Buddhism. Repudiation of excessive monastic influence is evident in laws enacted during the reign of the Emperor Kônin (reigned 770–781), and it was explicit under the succeeding reign of Kammu (782–805). Shortly after this latter ruler's accession, two agencies that had been set up specifically to promote the construction of monasteries and convents were summarily abolished. The power of the clergy accordingly decreased, but the final blow did not come until 794, when, as a part of a general governmental reform, the entire court was moved to what is now Kyoto, beyond the reach of pressure from the Nara monasteries.

As it turned out, the political loss to the church became a gain not for the imperial family, but for the nobility. One great and prolific family, the Fujiwara, soon established themselves as leaders, largely through the strategy of marrying daughters to a succession of emperors. After the tenth century a long series of Fujiwara regents and chancellors dominated both the court and the Kyoto aristocracy, but though the society over which they presided was brilliant, it was strongly inclined to become effete, and it was destined eventually to give way before more practical military barons from the provinces.

When deprived of imperial protection, Buddhist leaders had no one to fall back on but the nobility, and to make matters worse, the sects of Nara had become so dry and scholarly that they received little support from this class. As it happened, however, about this time young and energetic priests introduced the Tendai and Shingon sects from China, and these proved to be the solution to the Buddhist dilemma. Tendai teachings were brought from the continent in 804 by the monk Saichô, or Dengyô Daishi, as he was later known, who had been sent by the government to study. He and his followers established on Mt. Hiei, north of Kyoto, a monastery named the Enryaku-ji, which was to become one of the greatest cultural centers, as well as one of the strongest political forces, in Japanese history. Slightly later Kûkai, who under the name of Kôbô Daishi is now the most renowned of all Japanese monks, went to China, returned with the doctrines of the Shingon sect, and founded a monastry on Mt. Kôya known as the Kongôbu-ji.

Both Tendai and Shingon are based on intricate philosophical systems, but for all their cosmological exegetics, these "esoteric sects," as they are frequently called, reflect a remarkably practical frame of mind. According to theory, their form of worship is a means whereby the believer may enter into complete union with the infinite Buddha, but in practice it usually amounts to little more than a strict and detailed ritualism aimed at exorcism, the healing of illness, or the procurement of worldly goods. Many of the rituals are priestly secrets (hence the adjective "esoteric"), and that means, of course, that the benefits at which they are directed are unavailable to those who do not employ the clergy's aid. By the same token, however, little more than patronage of the priesthood is required of the believer. This is not to imply that there were no fervent believers among the followers of these sects. On the contrary, religious feeling seems to have been particularly strong during their period of dominance, although one must admit that it was deeply tinged with superstition. The point here, however, is that esotericism permitted those who so wished to adhere to their religion by proxy. It was no longer necessary for the ordinary Buddhist to worry about difficult philosophical problems or to observe ascetic rules. Naturally, this sort of religion appealed to the aristocracy, who were accustomed to ease and luxury, and as a consequence Mt. Hiei and Mt.

Figure 13. Miniature Shingon Pagoda of Early Type. Heian period.

Kôya began to receive the money that had formerly been used to build monasteries in Nara.

In China at this time there was a growing trend toward secluded mountain monasteries, and this was the case in Heian Japan as well. There were several reasons. One was that separation from the everyday world tended to remove ordinary temptations and to inspire contemplation. Another was that in the esoteric sects, priests held divine secrets that could not be passed on to just anyone, and it was desirable that they live largely by themselves. Furthermore, in Japan the founders of the new sects no doubt wished to avoid the excessive involvement with politics that had proved the downfall of the Nara clergy. Whatever the cause, the effect on architectural planning was tremendous. Only on level ground was it possible to erect a number of large pavilions in a regular pattern, as had previously been the practice. Instead, buildings now had to be arranged into small groups adapted to the natural surroundings. The Enryaku-ji itself was originally formed of three small compounds. The main hall was only about thirty feet wide by fifteen feet deep and was covered with a simple cypress-bark roof. Similarly, the hall dedicated to the Buddha Sakyamuni was only a tiny structure about eighteen feet square, roofed with boards.

Another change in the over-all form of monasteries was the adoption of a new type of living quarters for priests. Nara monasteries had had large dormitories around the lecture hall in which a number of monks lived together. Priests in esoteric establishments, however, lived in small separate dwellings, doubtless to facilitate private devotions and abstinence. These subsidiary structures, each of which had its tiny sanctuary, were scattered about in the neighborhood of the main buildings, from which they were architecturally independent *(Plate 91)*. In many cases they later split off and became branch monasteries.

An unusual type of pagoda is associated with the esoteric sects, particularly Shingon. Modeled on a picture in the Diamond Mandala, it had a round-topped cylindrical base surmounted by a roof like that of an ordinary pagoda *(Figure 13)*. In the earliest type there were auxiliary eaves around the lower circular portion, but later the space under these was enclosed and made part of the main structure. Consequently, in the fully developed form, only the very top of the round

Figure 14. The Diamond Mandala. Heian period.

portion shows above the first-floor roof. No examples have survived from the Heian period, but the one shown here *(Plate 92)*, which is from the Kamakura period, is recorded to have been patterned after a Heian model.

The esoteric sects also developed a new type for the principal sanctuary. In the Nara period main halls had been designed as in China with the idea that the worshiper would perform his devotions outside. As a result, they were comparatively shallow, and the central Buddha was visible from without *(Figure 9)*. At times, however, a separate hall of worship had been erected in front, and eventually this was incorporated into the main building to form a deeper structure known as a "double hall" *(sôdô)*, of which examples seem to have existed in the late Nara period. Presumably this came about simply because of a need for shelter, but the esoteric Buddhists perceived that a long, darkened interior created a mystic effect eminently suitable to their beliefs, and they adopted the double hall for their monasteries. Its two sections were later unified under a single hipped and gabled roof, so that the division between them was not immediately apparent from the exterior. Most often the sanctum was five bays deep and the outer hall of worship two. With certain exceptions, this structure was adopted even by non-esoteric sects during and after the Kamakura period, and it ultimately became the fixed style for Japanese temples. The principal building of the Kanshin-ji *(Plate 94)* is a fourteenth-century example.

One of the most remarkable features of Heian art is the abundance of Buddhist paintings. The main reason for this seems to be a greatly increased emphasis on painting on the part of the new Buddhist sects. Nara Buddhists had had temples constructed and statues carved in the hope of obtaining a favorable transmigration, but followers of esotericism occupied themselves instead with semi-magical rituals designed to produce concrete benefits. For each of the ceremonies an altar had to be set up and decorated in a particular way. The central icon varied with the purpose of the service, and, in principle, a new one had to be used each time. Obviously, this entailed an ever-growing number of images, and practical considerations resulted in a preference for paintings over statues.

One may also observe a distinct change in the prevailing types of Buddhist pictures. Two new varieties became especially prominent. The first was a diagram called a mandala *(Figure 14)*, which was an attempt to represent visually the obscure and intricate cosmological concepts of esotericism. This unpromising task did not stimulate originality of artistic expression, since it amounted to little more than copying in a set pattern a hierarchy of cosmic beings, sometimes running into the hundreds. Nevertheless, the strict discipline imposed on the draftsmen led to certain technical advances.

More rewarding than these geometrical exercises was the other new type of picture, in which beings of wrathful aspect appeared as separate images. Most common were the "twelve guardian deities," and the "enlightened kings," among the latter of whom Fudô Myô-ô (Acalanatha) was particularly prominent. In theory, these gods, absorbed into Buddhism from Hinduism and other religions, were benevolent protectors of the faith, but in order to frighten its physical and spiritual enemies they revealed themselves in terrifying forms. Most of them had it within their power to grant specific benefits to those who performed rituals before them, and the superstitious Buddhists of the Heian period took up their various cults with a vengeance. As a consequence, whereas they had

formerly been seen merely as attendants to Buddhas and other higher members of the cosmic order, they now became the central objects of worship in many religious ceremonies. The most famous picture of a wrathful god is perhaps the one known as the "Red Fudô," which is housed in a temple on Mt. Kôya *(Plate 4)*.

Not all of the miscellaneous deities held sacred by the esoteric Buddhists appeared so angry. Like Fudô, Kujaku Myô-ô, (Mahamayuri) is one of the "enlightened kings," but he is always shown in a very benevolent mood. The example given *(Plate 5)* is from the late Heian period, when brilliant colors and gorgeous ornamentation were the rule in Buddhist paintings. Despite a tendency toward decorativeness, however, there is still a certain air of solidity in this painting, as can be seen by comparing it with a contemporary image of the Bodhisattva Fugen (Samantabhadra), in

Figure 15. Chinese Sandalwood Statue. Sung period.

which feminine delicacy and ornateness are carried to an extreme *(Plate 6)*.

The iconographical features of all these esoteric deities, whether wrathful or benign, were prescribed by canon, and in learning to draw them correctly, artists spent years copying black-and-white outline models from China. No doubt the proficiency they gained from this practice fostered the development of the ink monochrome, particularly the type in which line was the principal element.

Buddhist sculpture during the Heian period was as much affected by the rise of esotericism as were painting and architecture. More images were made than before, and the tendency was to favor wooden over dry-lacquer and clay statuary, which involved elaborate processes and, in the case of the former, expensive materials. The location of monasteries in the midst of mountain forests strengthened this tendency, as did the growing appreciation of sandalwood images that were being imported from China *(Figure 15)*. From this period on, Japanese sculpture was almost entirely of wood.

During the early Heian, the technique for making wooden statues was as yet primitive. The main portions of the image were carved in one piece and projecting limbs or objects held in the hands added later. When the material was sandalwood, which is very hard and fine-grained, everything, including even the ornaments, was carved from a single block. The statue of Yakushi in the Jingo-ji *(Plate 57)*, strictly speaking, may not, be a specimen of esoteric Buddhist sculpture, but it will serve as an example. The whole image was sharply chiseled from a single piece of sandalwood. In accordance with current fashions, the body of the Buddha is corpulent, and the expression on his face is stern. The spirit of the statue is, as a result, austere and majestic.

Originally the native Shinto religion had had no icons whatever, but from the Nara period on there was a growing tendency for it to merge with Buddhism, and the influence of the latter led to the creation of Shinto images. The example shown here *(Plate 58)* is one of the oldest known. Like contemporary Buddhist statues, it is carved from one block and is characterized by massiveness and force.

In the tenth and eleventh centuries, esoteric Buddhism began to be displaced by a new cult known as Pure Land Buddhism, whose followers believed that the Buddha Amida would transport all those who invoked his name to his "Pure Land," or paradise. Properly speaking, we cannot say that this faith was novel to Heian Japan, for it had existed in the Asuka and Nara periods, and, indeed had furnished the subject for one of the Hôryû-ji murals. However, believers in Amida, or "Amidists," as they are sometimes called, did not begin to organize separate sects until mid-Heian times.

The rise of Amidism at this point is not difficult to explain. One of the doctrines common to all Japanese Buddhist sects was that two thousand years after the demise of the Buddha Sakyamuni the world would enter a five-hundred-year period of degeneration, after which it would be destroyed. It so happened that by contemporary calculations the two-thousandth anniversary of Sakyamuni's death fell in 1051, and consequently, the next year was taken to be the beginning of the disastrous half-millenium. The fact that economic and political conditions were gradually moving from bad to worse during the late Heian no doubt lent credibility to the theory, and it began to be taken more and more seriously. Into a society troubled with such thoughts of destruction, there came the great priest Hônen, who offered a simple remedy for salvation. Cutting through a tangled web of philosophical speculation and priestly hocus-pocus in which esoteric Buddhism had become ensnared, he taught that to gain Buddhahood one had but to utter the name of Amida Buddha with sincere faith in his saving powers. This uncomplicated doctrine was eagerly accepted by a large proportion of the population, and from the twelfth century until the present the Amidist faith has been the most typical form of Japanese Buddhism.

The nobility seem to have been as much attracted by the Pure Land faith as the masses, but it is not at all certain that all of them grasped the spirit of it. At least a few appear to have got the notion that it would be more pleasant to have paradise here on earth than to wait until one died and could be reborn there. Members of the Fujiwara and other wealthy clans set up private temples that, in so far as available riches would permit, reproduced the Pure Land. The buildings were grand and glorious palaces, luxuriously decorated throughout, especially in and around the sancta. The greatest of these man-made heavens was the Hôjô-ji, built by the all-powerful Chancellor Fujiwara Michinaga (966–1027). It no longer exists, but a history of the Fujiwara family says in speaking of it: "Michinaga set up so many halls that one seemed to see the Pure Land here before one's eyes." A pavilion dedicated to Amida and housing nine large statues of him was the most ornate of the separate buildings.

Nobles spent day after day in seclusion in such temples, calling upon the Buddha's name and abandoning themselves to religious ecstasy. At ceremonies in the northwest hall of the Hôjô-ji handsome young boys would be picked from among the priests, clad in lavish robes, and set to repeating the invocation to Amida, or *nembutsu,* as it is usually called. In 1024 Michinaga held a "myriad-lights ceremony," for which he had innumerable lanterns made of gold, silver, and precious stones in the most elaborate fashion known to contemporary craftsmen. A century or so later, Taira no Shigemori built a hall twelve bays square to enshrine forty-eight statues of Amida. Two young ladies were placed in attendance on each icon, while a third took care of the night-lamp before it. After sunset the attendants donned ornate clothing and walked around the hall reciting the *nembutsu.* Later they formed a procession in groups of sixes and paraded about sounding gongs and singing. From literary records of such goings-on, one supposes that the atmosphere in these temples was highly diverting. Apparently, the nobles used them as places of entertainment, albeit a very special kind of entertainment.

In the monasteries of the age, the hall of Amida was usually the most important building. As a rule, it was a square structure with a sanctum one bay square in the center, surrounded by a space in which worshipers might perform the rite of circumambulation. The simplest halls were only three bays square *(Figure 16),* but some of the more ambitious ones were tremendous. A type housing nine statues of Amida, one for each level of his paradise, was fairly common. Such edifices were oblong, usually eleven or thirteen bays in width and much less in depth.

The most remarkable Heian temple to Amida still standing is the Phoenix Hall of the Byôdô-in *(Plate 90),* a magnificent monastery erected by the regent Fujiwara Yorimichi (992–1074) in 1052 on land that had been part of his country villa. Although not nearly so large as some other buildings of its type this hall is more elaborate than most. Modeled on a sacred palace that appears in representations of Amida's paradise, it has a central pavilion on either side of which extend wings terminating in small towers. As has been aptly remarked, the entire building seems like a great bird poised to take flight. The central structure is only three bays by two. Inside, it has a highly ornate adytum one bay square in which is enshrined a famous image of Amida, to be described in more detail below. Outside, there are auxiliary eaves supported by slender columns that give a graceful lift to the structure. By contrast, the thicker columns supporting the wings seem steadier and add to the stability of the façade. The exterior was originally painted red and must have made a dazzling sight reflected in the pond that lies directly before the hall.

Figure 16. Small Amida Hall and Typical Sanctum.

It appears that Shinto continued to exist during the Nara and Heian periods largely on the sufferance of Buddhism. When the foreign religion had first been introduced, it had had to accommodate itself to the native faith in order to survive, but after a time this situation had been reversed. The great Shinto establishments at Ise and Izumo managed to remain fairly free of Buddhist influence, but they were exceptions. Buddhists and Shintoists alike accepted a syncretic doctrine whereby it was held that the myriad nature deities of Shinto were but local manifestations of the universal Buddhas. This theory, known as *honchi suijaku*, or "manifestation in this land," led to visual representations of the Shinto gods, mentioned above, and a number of other changes in Shinto art. Shrines came to be painted in bright colors and covered with curving roofs, the eaves of which were supported by brackets. Two-story gateways were sometimes built in front in place of the traditional torii, and often the surrounding fences were replaced by corridors. There also appeared a type of shrine building that was akin to the double-hall Buddhist temple mentioned above. Still, however, Shinto architecture tended to be conservative. During this period there developed a shrine form that has since become the most popular of all. It consisted of nothing more than a one-room building with a surrounding porch and a gabled roof, one eave of which was greatly elongated to cover the entrance.

No example of reside..tial architecture from this period remains, but from pertinent documents it appears that the basic structure for the dwellings of nobles was an oblong rectangular building with a gabled roof, augmented by lean-tos *(Figure 17)*. By the addition of corridors and auxiliary apartments more or less like those of the Phoenix Hall *(Plate 90)*, the central structure was expanded into a large rambling mansion. The doors were composed of two parts, the lower removable and the upper attached by hinges at the top so as to open outwards. The floors were almost entirely of wood. Buildings of this type are described as *shinden*, or literally "sleeping palaces." They were often surrounded by vast gardens which reproduced famous landscapes in miniature.

The sponsoring of great monasteries by rich nobles had an interesting effect on the status of sculptors. Hitherto, large temples had been built under the supervision of a government office established especially for that purpose, and this office had contained a bureau in charge of the artists appointed to make statues. Around the middle of the Heian period, however, the "family" monasteries began to employ individual sculptors to work for them exclusively. Many of the artists entered the priesthood and received ranks in the Buddhist hierarchy. The first known to have been so honored was Jôchô, who made the central icon for the Phoenix Hall. In 1022 he was given the priestly rank of *Hokkyô*, or "Bridge of the Law," in recognition of the skill he had displayed in carving statues for the Hôjô-ji. The precedent was

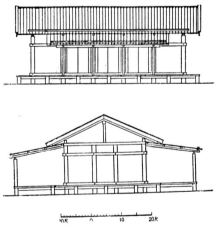

Figure 17. Reconstruction of a Nara Palace Building of the Type from which the Shinden *Style Developed.*

followed in later years, and some outstanding artists were promoted to the highest honorific ranks accorded to priests.

Simultaneously, another institutional change took place in the field of sculpture. Instead of working in government buildings or in temples, sculptors began to open private studios, a development made possible largely by a technical innovation. Whereas in earlier times wooden images had as a rule been carved in one piece, they were now usually being made in parts and assembled. This allowed not only for more careful and ornate carving, but also for a sort of mass production. Needless to say, some of the force of the single-block method was lost, but this could hardly have been considered a drawback by the Heian nobles, much of whose time and mental effort was in any case devoted to concealing the rude facts of life in a cloud of inconsequential décor. The credit for bringing the new technique to perfection belongs to Jôchô, whose stylistic principles were followed by most subsequent Japanese sculptors. The impressive statue of Amida in the Phoenix Hall *(Plate 59),* which he made in 1053, became the classic form for Japanese Buddhas. Produced in sections, it reveals loving attention to even the smallest details. The diminutive, regularly arranged curls of hair, the straight hairline, the relatively small nose and mouth, the benign face, the slender but well-rounded arms, and the flowing drapery are all typical of this age of delicacy, but the statue does not share that quality of irresoluteness often observed in contemporaneous works. Jôchô himself was able to endow the Heian ideal with a certain realism and strength, derived from the orthodox style of the Nara period. His followers, however, were not so talented. In copying him, they all too frequently sought only for prettiness and grace, and their works tend as a result to be flaccid and spiritless.

The statue just mentioned illustrates the most important single trend of the Heian period, that is, the departure from Chinese models. Aside from those features that are more or less universal in Buddhist statues, there is virtually no resemblance between this Amida and Chinese prototypes. The face, the over-all composition, the setting, and the incidental decorations are all distinctly Japanese, and so, indeed, is the religion that inspired the statue, for although Amidism had existed in China since early times, it had never had the force and popularity that it had in Japan in this age. In China the spread of the Pure Land faith was only a tangential movement. In Japan, however, it was a protestant reformation that pushed the earlier forms of Buddhism into the background once and for all, at least as far as the masses were concerned.

The religious divergence between Japan and China was only one sign of what was happening during this era. It would probably not be too much to say that in the Asuka and Nara periods nothing important had been done without a Chinese precedent, but after the third or fourth decade of the ninth century the situation began to change. There were many reasons. For one thing, after 750 the economic foundation of the house of T'ang weakened, and with it went political authority. China tended more and more to separate into autonomous local states, and there were at least two serious rebellions. In 906 the T'ang fell in name as well as in fact. From then until the establishment of the Sung Dynasty in 960, conditions were chaotic. Central governments were set up by five short-lived dynasties, but none of them controlled as much as half of the nation, nor could any put an end to civil warfare. The Chinese of this period consequently had little in the way of cultural guidance to offer to the Japanese. At the same time, in Japan, because of ever-increasing tax exemptions to monasteries and nobles, the government was finding it harder and harder to meet its internal needs, let alone finance expensive expeditions to the Chinese court. After 839 there were no more official missions, and in 894 it was formally decided not to send more. Official exchanges between the Japanese and Chinese governments were not resumed until 1077, and they were quite sporadic for more than a century after that. During this interval of isolation from the continent, Japan remade the culture that had been brought from China. The Chinese-style political system was retained in name, but the actual work of government was carried on by organs that were essentially Japanese in origin. Similarly, lip service was paid to the ancient Chinese principle of equal landholdings and taxes, but thanks to the processes of commendation and benefice, feudalism in a near-European sense was coming steadily closer. In literature, the vernacular was beginning to regain its rightful place, after having been all but replaced by Chinese. Even the Chinese ideographs

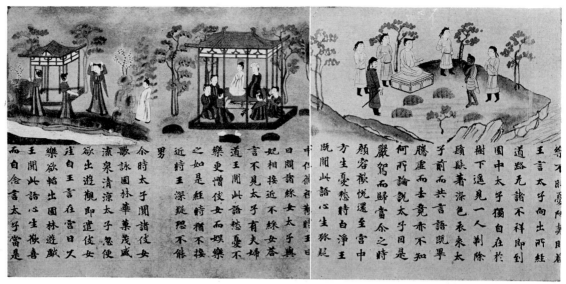

Figure 18. Sections of the Illustrated Sutra on Cause and Effect. *Nara period.*

were being supplemented by a native syllabary. These changes were not necessarily all to the good, but they bear witness to a refreshing spirit of self-assertion on the part of the Japanese.

The most significant artistic development during this period was the appearance of a completely Japanese style of painting. Hints of it can be seen in the brilliant color, the elaborate decoration, and the lyric air of contemporary Buddhist paintings *(Plate 6)*, but it is far more conspicuous in secular works. We have mentioned before that the mansions of the Nara nobles had been decorated with secular paintings in a Chinese style. Now, pictures on walls and sliding doors became more frequent, and following the general movement of the times, they tended to depart increasingly from Chinese modes. It is impossible to say at what point they ceased to be Chinese and became Japanese, but the term *yamato-e*, or "Japanese painting," is seen in a writing dated 999, and its appearance indicates that the new style was by that time at least sufficiently distinct to have received a name of its own. *Yamato-e* stands in contrast to *kara-e*, which means "Chinese painting." The latter is used to refer to works in Chinese styles by Japanese artists, as well as to Japanese renditions of Chinese subjects. *Yamato-e*, on the other hand, is applied to typically Japanese scenes painted in Japanese fashion.

Two or three early *yamato-e* screen paintings have been preserved, and from the stylistic point of view they show a general inclination toward a more gentle, intimate approach than is common in Chinese works. The characteristics of the *yamato-e*, however, are displayed much more clearly in the rare and precious scroll paintings that have come down to us from the Heian period. It is likely that these developed in some devious way from illustrated sutra scrolls of the Nara period *(Figure 18)*, but now the subjects were literary rather than religious. The most important of the early picture scrolls is a set composed of excerpts from the famous *Tale of Genji (Plate 7)* interspersed with illustrative paintings. There is virtually no action in the latter, the incidents described apparently having been chosen from among those that could best be represented with "still" pictures. The story centers around the Heian court, and in particular around the love adventures of the rich, handsome, and thoroughly appealing Prince Genji. Appropriately, the paintings are executed in sumptuous color and with quiet, unhurried lines. The faces of the characters are drawn in symbolic fashion, with mere slits for eyes and diminutive hooks for noses. They are exceedingly expressionless, but somehow they evoke sympathy. All the scenes shown in the illustrations are viewed at an angle from above, as is almost invariably true in later works of the type. When the scene is set inside a building, the roof is omitted, the resulting form being what the Japanese call literally a "house with the roof blown off" *(fukinuke yatai) (Figure 19)*.

In addition to picture scrolls of this sort, attention should be called to the colorful *yamato-e* paintings that adorned Buddhist sutras during this period. It was common for the nobles to donate handsome, expensively decorated sutra scrolls to shrines and temples, and usually there was a painting at the beginning of each *(Plate 8)*. In the existing examples, the pictures usually had little or no connection with the subject of the sutra. Ordinarily they were brilliant genre paintings of the same type that appeared in the literary scrolls. As time went on, however, the *yamato-e* style came to be used in depicting religious stories, particularly the biographies of famous priests and the histories of temples. A masterpiece in this category is the set of scrolls entitled "The History of Mt. Shigi" *(Plate 9)*, which tells of miraculous events in the life of a priest named Myôren. This is probably more or less contemporary with the Genji scrolls, but it is very different in style. Instead of dreamlike splendor, it is marked by vitality and dynamic force. The action is so complete that the text of the story is all but superfluous. Separate incidents are accordingly not divided by explanatory passages, and instead of a series of vignettes, there is a continual story, unfolding chronologically from right to left. From a technical point of view it may be noted that the sense of movement given by this painting results from sparing use of color and from wonderfully articulate ink lines. The complete mastery of line demonstrated here is the result of a long historical development. For centuries painter-priests had been copying and re-copying black-and-white outline patterns for esoteric Buddhist images. By this time all conceivable types of linear brushwork had been thoroughly incorporated into painting traditions, and trained artists must have been able to draw lines such as those seen here almost without looking.

Even more delightful are the free linear patterns in the "Frolic of the Animals" *(Plates 10 and 11)*. This celebrated work is attributed to the Archbishop Kakuyû (1053–1140), or, as he is better known, the Bishop of Toba, but the attribution is unproven. The latter two of the four scrolls appear to date from a considerably later period than the others, and they were almost certainly drafted by a different artist. The original painting is thought to have been a satire in which animals behave as humans, but even this is uncertain. If, indeed, satire was intended, it appears to have been of the playful rather than the biting variety. Some of the scenes appear to be irreverent, if not malicious, jibes at the Buddhist monastic orders, but many others seem to be nothing more nor less than pictures of romping animals. In any event, the buoyancy and effortlessness of the ink lines make this one of the most charming of all Japanese paintings.

During the Heian period the development of the crafts was more quantitative than qualitative. The output of ceramic wares increased greatly, and manufacture spread to many of the outlying provinces. Kilns later to become famous were established in the provinces of Bizen, Ômi, Tamba, and Owari. The Seto area in the last named province, for instance, was so intimately connected with the subsequent development of ceramic wares in Japan that its name is now applied generally to them.

Almost no samples of Heian textiles have been preserved, but the *yamato-e* paintings of the period furnish a certain amount of information about them. There was a pronounced trend away from the Chinese-style clothing that had been worn by Nara aristocrats. Both women's and men's apparel *(Figure 20)* became fuller and longer, and pleats and folds naturally became deeper. The formal outfit for women was a very unique one now popularly called the "twelve-layer dress." It con-

Figure 19. Fukinuke Yatai.

Figure 20. Nobleman Clad in Typical Heian Garment.

sisted of numerous layers of undergarments in various colors, a long pleated outer skirt that spread out broadly in the back, and an outer robe made of an especially beautiful fabric. There were set combinations for the colors of the undergarments, and beauty was sought in the harmony of these shades, which were visible at the collar, sleeves, and foot, rather than in surface patterns. Accordingly, there was a trend in this period toward solid colors. Batik and stencil-dyed patterns nearly disappeared, while woven or embroidered designs became smaller and more geometrical than in the Nara period. It might be noted in passing that the common people of this age wore a garment that very much resembled the modern kimono in form, though not in quality. Contemporary picture scrolls indicate that plebeian dress was frequently decorated with large, free surface patterns, probably either drawn or printed with molds.

The craft that showed the most remarkable progress during this era was that of lacquer manufacture. Almost all of the techniques mastered during the Nara period were preserved, and most of them were improved, but there were certain notable changes. For one thing, as in the case of sculpture, the dry-lacquer method was dropped in

favor of wood. Also, designs made by sprinkling gold dust *(maki-e)* almost completely replaced those made with gold paint or sheet gold. At the same time, the technique of decorating lacquer ware with inlaid mother-of-pearl came to be employed widely and effectively. The cosmetics box shown here *(Plate 79)* is a beautiful example of the high technical level reached by Heian lacquer-makers. The design is made partly of gold dust, partly of a lighter powder composed of both gold and silver, and partly of mother-of-pearl; the background has a light sprinkling of relatively coarse gold powder. The design is tasteful and well balanced—quite simple in appearance despite the costliness of the materials with which it was made.

The fame of Japanese lacquer spread overseas. Japanese monks who traveled to China during this age customarily took a good deal of it to use as gifts, and it was praised in a number of contemporary Chinese sources. The techniques for making it had of course been imported from China, but the Japanese products now surpassed those of China in quality. Apparently some of the methods had been completely forgotten abroad. One Chinese source says, for instance, that mother-of-pearl articles "come originally from Japan."

The Heian period was an age of reaction, but reaction in a healthy sense. Japan had derived incalculable benefits from the close imitation of China that had marked the Asuka and Nara periods, but imitation could not go on forever. Much of what had been imported had ceased to have any meaning whatever. The bureaucratic administrative system with its coveted ranks and titles, for example, was nothing more than a great ornament that added to the glamor of the capital city, but not to its ability to control the provinces. The Chinese-style metropolis was itself in many ways no more than an ornament. It had grown economically and politically remote from the areas of production, and its ruling class had retreated into that completely incredible world portrayed in their picture-scrolls and novels. For all this, however, Kyoto continued to function as the center of culture, or at least of what everyone considered to be culture, since what went on in the outlying areas did not count as that even to the people who lived there. Literature and art, if not religion as well, were virtually confined to the capital, and while they were correspondingly limited in scope,

they were neither stagnant nor oppressively imita-
tive. Late Heian art is open to the charge of weak-
ness and over-refinement, but it is original. Had
the Heian aristocracy allowed itself to become
infected with the vigorous spirit abroad in the
provinces, they might have produced an art of
more universal significance, but even so they
succeeded in creating something quite new and
pleasing. In their hands, Japanese art for the first
time became Japanese.

V. THE KAMAKURA PERIOD
1185 — 1338

It was hardly to be expected that the elegant but
impractical nobles of the Heian period could con-
tinue to hold political power indefinitely. They
were almost completely impotent in the military
sense, and they were forced to rely increasingly
on alliances with provincial warrior chieftains.
These were in many instances cadet members of
noble families, and for a time they remained
content to fight out the political battles of their
betters in Kyoto, but eventually the more ambitious
among them began to aspire for greater power.
For some time there was a bitter struggle for
control between the Minamoto and Taira families,
with the Fujiwara choosing sides as the occasion
seemed to demand. The conflict came to a head
during the 1150's, and the Taira won out. They
thereupon took over the government from the
Fujiwara, but it appears that although they were
a military clan, their way of life was hardly better
suited to reality than that of their predecessors.
Less than twenty years after Taira no Kiyomori
(1118–1181) had established himself as Chancellor
of the Empire, his faction was forced to yield to
the Minamoto. In 1192 Minamoto no Yoritomo
(1147–1199) became the "Great Barbarian-Subdu-
ing General," that is, the shogun, and promptly
set up in the eastern town of Kamakura a military
government that henceforth ruled the country
in fact though not in name. After the third
Minamoto shogun the Kamakura government
passed under the control of regents from the Hôjô
family, and the shogunate, like the court before
it, became more fictional than real, but the regency
continued to rule largely in the tradition of Yoritomo and was on the whole a successful administration. In the late thirteenth century it survived
two attempted invasions by Mongols from the
continent, but was so weakened by them that it
was overthrown in 1333, shortly after which the
Ashikaga family, an offshoot of the Minamoto,
set up a new shogunate in the Muromachi district
of Kyoto.

The cruel strife between the Minamoto and
Taira, which lasted throughout the latter half of
the twelfth century, led to widespread disillusion-
ment with the present world and hope for a better
one in the afterlife. As a consequence, the Pure
Land faith spread even more rapidly than before,
and the widespread longing for paradise became
more urgent. This development is quite clearly
reflected in contemporary art. During the former
era, when the nobles had been so worldly as to
try reproducing Amida's paradise on earth, the
Buddha had usually been shown quietly ensconced
at the center of heaven and surrounded by lesser
beings. Now, however, he mounts a soaring cloud
and descends with his attendants to greet the
believer on earth. Action and vigor mark the scene.
Evidently the people of this age were too realistic
to be content with a Buddha who did nothing
but look serene. When they called out to him,
they wanted him to do something about it, and
quickly. With the passage of time, however, a
different trend appeared. Sweetness and grace
replaced vitality. The typical Pure Land painting
of the late Kamakura era shows Amida rising
beyond a range of mountains and looking com-
passionately down upon the present world. He
is the soul of beauty, and his figure is richly
adorned with gold and silver. To his hand are
attached cords intended for the believer to hold
while in prayer, in the hope of being led away
to paradise. The idea behind the painting is sentimental, and the image itself is shallow.

When the Amidists set about propagating their
faith, they attempted not only to attract men by
showing the infinite beauties of paradise, but also
to frighten them with hideous alternatives. Accord-

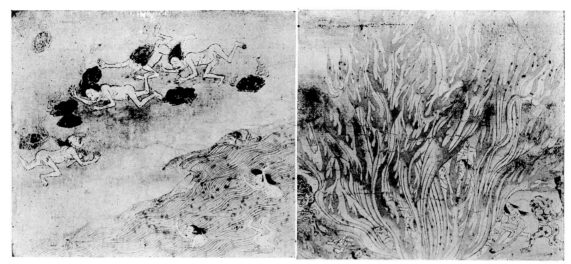

Figure 21. Sections from the "Handbook on Hells." Kamakura period.

ing to Buddhist lore there are six realms in which sentient beings can transmigrate. They are, in ascending order, that of the infernal hells, that of hungry ghosts, that of beasts, that of demonic spirits, that of humans, and that of lesser deities. The Kamakura flair for vivid expression found an ideal outlet in representations of these, particularly the ones in the subhuman classes. The verve with which the ghosts, beasts, and demons are portrayed sometimes leads one to suspect that artists enjoyed them much more than the ethereal, and often saccharine, Buddhas. Hells and purgatories were the subject of a number of scroll paintings *(Figure 21)*. The one from which a section is reproduced here *(Plate 12)* deals with the sufferings of humans rather than with the more fanciful tortures of the lesser beings, but it has the same liveliness and vigor.

The Kamakura period was the age of the scroll painting, no doubt because this form was ideal for depicting action. Beautifully colored "still" pictures, like those in the Genji scrolls, were still made, but lively works in the tradition of the "History of Mt. Shigi" *(Plate 9)* were more common, and synthetic paintings having the coloring of the one but the movement of the other were the most typical of all. A classic example is "The Story of Tomo no Dainagon," of which a small section is presented here *(Plate 13)*.

The Kamakura picture scrolls dealt with a variety of subjects. Aside from using this medium to depict the terrors of hell, the Buddhists continued to employ it for telling the stories of great

priests, famous temples, and occasionally famous Shinto shrines. Some of these works ran to forty or fifty scrolls, and many exist in a number of different versions, but although religious scrolls were turned out in great quantity, the scroll remained, as in the Heian period, more closely associated with secular literature. Shown here are examples of the two main types. The first is from an illustrated version of the *Pillow Book* of Sei Shônagon *(Plate 14)*. This painting is practically an ink monochrome, the only color being the red applied to the lips of the characters, but it is very different from lively monochromes like the "Frolic of the Animals." The lines are as tranquil as those of the Genji scrolls, and they function only as contours.

The "Pillow Book" also resembles the Genji scrolls in that there is virtually no action. In strong contrast to these scenes from court life is a large class of works inspired by medieval sagas of battle, of which "The Latter Three Years' Campaign" *(Plate 15)* is typical. The "Mt. Shigi" style was naturally found more suitable to these tales of war.

There was a general trend toward compactness in Kamakura scrolls, and the subject was viewed from a more distant point in space than before. Faces became longer, and the slit-like eyes were made somewhat more realistic by the addition of pupils. The principal change from the Heian period, however, was the greatly increased emphasis on movement and speed.

Thanks, no doubt, to the realistic spirit of the

times, there appeared during this epoch a group of paintings that can be classed as true portraits. Previously there had existed many likenesses of Buddhist patriarchs and priests, but these were as a rule intended for worship, and consequently inclined strongly toward idealization. Non-religious sketches of real people were probably made during the Heian, but the earliest known samples are four portraits from the early Kamakura period now preserved in the Jingo-ji. The most famous one, which is shown here, is a picture of the shogun Minamoto no Yoritomo *(Plate 16)*. It has neither the sacred air of Buddhist portraits nor the abstract expression found so frequently in pictures of historical personages. On the contrary, something about this portrait *is* Yoritomo. The artist, Fujiwara Takanobu (1142–1205), clearly wished to paint an objective likeness of his subject. The somewhat later portrait of Kôbô Daishi as a boy *(Plate 17)* was probably intended as an object of worship, but still the face is more accurately and painstakingly portrayed than in the religious portraits of other ages.

Alongside the comparatively realistic portraits already mentioned, highly impressionistic likenesses in the *yamato-e* style were also in fashion during this period *(Plate 18)*. These are very sketchy, but many of them succeed admirably in summing up the subject's main characteristics in a few hasty strokes. In this age there also appeared portraits of priests that showed the influence of a style popular in China during the Sung period *(Figure 22)*. These last remind us that official contact with China had been renewed, and that a new wave of Chinese culture was beginning to be felt.

The influence of China was first seen in the field of architecture. Very shortly after the beginning of the Kamakura period the Tôdaiji, which had been destroyed by fire in 1180, was reconstructed under the direction of the priest Chôgen. Chôgen had made three trips to China, during which he had supervised the building of several monasteries there, and in rebuilding the Tôdaiji he was able to use the latest continental techniques. The buildings he set up were in a massive style known to the Japanese as the "Indian style" *(tenjiku-yô)*, but having no real connection with India. It is marked by the use of cantilever-style eave brackets and fan rafters. The Indian style was not very popular in Japan, and there are few examples of it left today. Of all the Tôdaiji build-

Figure 22. Portrait of the Priest Kôshô. Kamakura period.

ings only the main gateway remains *(Figure 23)*.

Around the beginning of the thirteenth century, Zen Buddhism began to take hold in Japan, no doubt because its simple creed of direct enlightenment appealed to the unphilosophical warrior class. Associated with this religion was a new kind of architecture which in opposition to the Indian style is called the "Chinese style" *(kara-yô)*, and which is exemplified by the reliquary hall in the Engaku-ji at Kamakura *(Plate 93)*. In the Chinese style, brackets were placed not only atop pillars but in between them as well, so that the space under the rafters often is filled with woodwork. The style is also distinguished by steep roofs and prominent curved lines (as, for example, in the window casings). Zen monasteries of the Kamakura period almost invariably followed this pattern.

By this time the architectural types imported during the Nara period had become so standard that they were given the name "Japanese style" (wa-yô) to distinguish them from the two newer varieties. As a matter of fact, most buildings during this period were built in some combination of the three styles mentioned. At first Japanese and Indian were mixed, and later Japanese and Chinese. In the end, elements of all three were to be found in most Buddhist buildings.

Chinese influence is also evident in the sculpture of the Kamakura period, though not so much as in architecture. Specifically, there was a new element of realism that came from Sung works, and it was accentuated by a concurrent revival of Nara modes, which themselves were on the whole realistic. The most famous sculptor of the period was Unkei, one of whose mature works is shown here (Plate 61). As can be seen from this example, Unkei did not depart completely from Heian tradition, but he added a good deal of vigor to it. He was succeeded by his three sons, of whom the most talented was Kôben. Kôben's image of Tentô-ki (Plate 62) and the statue of Basu (Plate 63) by his elder brother Tankei are both excellent examples of the dynamic force that marked Unkei's school.

The emergence of the warrior class as the leading stratum of society brought about a number of changes in the practical arts. Swords and arms took on a new importance, and during the Kamakura and Muromachi periods Japanese swordmakers developed methods that have never since been surpassed. The weapons they produced were exported to China in their own time and today are highly prized by collectors everywhere.

As a rule, the Kamakura warrior-rulers pre-

Figure 24. Fabric with Design of Phoenixes and Mallow Blossoms. Kamakura period.

ferred simpler clothing than that of the idle Heian aristocracy. The many layers of garments worn by women were gradually shed, and the voluminous folds in men's clothing gave way to more form-fitting styles. The over-all trend in apparel for both men and women was toward a robe that differs little from the modern kimono. There was consequently renewed emphasis on surface patterns, but these remained relatively conservative in both scale and color. The usual design was some

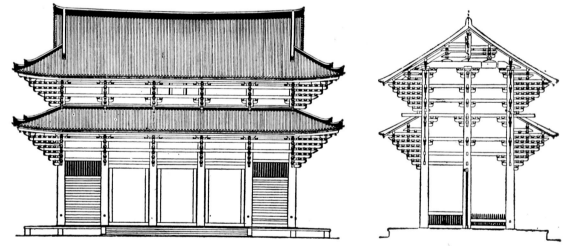

Figure 23. Elevation of the Main Gateway of the Tôdaiji. Kamakura period.

simple combination of birds and flowers *(Figure 24)*, embroidered or colored by the tie-dyeing method. To tell the truth, the textile craft was at a relatively low level, and it remained so until the Muromachi period, when the importation of fine fabrics from Ming China inspired new improvements.

For the most part ceramics had declined during the latter part of the Heian period, but a few of the kilns remained active. As intimated before, the Seto kilns in Owari showed outstanding progress. They were greatly influenced by porcelain brought from Sung China, and the same was more or less true of the other kilns. The discovery of innumerable fragments of Sung celadon in the vicinities of Kamakura and the Kyushu ports of trade indicates that Chinese wares were in common use, at least among the upper classes.

VI. THE MUROMACHI PERIOD
1 3 3 8 — 1 5 7 3

In 1338 Ashikaga Takauji (1305–1358), who had succeeded in bringing the greater part of the country under his military control, founded a new shogunate. His clan continued to rule as shoguns for the succeeding two and a half centuries, which are known to art historians as the Muromachi period, but during much of that time their authority was exceedingly tenuous. The first sixty years were troubled by a bitter dispute over the imperial succession, and the last century witnessed continual civil war and social upheaval. In the intervening years, however, there were two or three fairly strong shoguns, under whose rule a number of interesting developments took place. Most important from our point of view perhaps was the opening of trade with Ming China by Ashikaga Yoshimitsu (1358–1408), the third shogun. This step heightened the influence of China on Japanese life and served to stimulate renewed progress in the arts and crafts. Chinese paintings, Chinese ceramics, and even Chinese clothing enjoyed a new vogue, nor was it limited to the Kyoto area, for powerful local lords and great monasteries engaged independently in traffic with the Chinese court.

Most of the military magnates quite accurately judged themselves too unlettered to take personal charge of diplomatic exchanges with China, and this, coupled with their affinity for Zen Buddhism, led them to entrust the actual negotiations to Zen priests. These latter composed messages, acted as couriers, and at times even prepared the financial accounts entailed in commercial interchanges. It is not surprising, therefore, that Zen canons of taste are reflected in the art objects that were brought from China in this era. Furthermore, since Zen priests also in many instances served as cultural advisers to the feudal barons, including the shogun, their aesthetic principles were accepted in the seignorial manor as well as in the monastery.

Among the most prominent artistic imports were magnificent ink monochromes painted by Sung artists such as Tung Yüan, Ma Yüan, and Hsia Kuei. These were frequently hung in the halls of Zen monasteries, where they were regarded as guides to enlightenment, and, in fact, many of them, particularly those of the priest-painters Mu Ch'i and Liang K'ai, had been intended as that. Compact and succinct, the new paintings had an instantaneous impact on the viewer, like that of a sudden insight. Their abbreviated, almost abstract, black lines seemed to contain the ultimate secret of nature—the Truth that brought deliverance from a world of delusion. Even to the non-mystic, the quiet, uncluttered atmosphere that pervaded the black-and-white drawings must have conveyed a profound sense of peace.

The first Japanese known to have imitated the Sung monochromes were all Zen priests to whom art was more or less a hobby. Many of them, however, were exceedingly talented, and some so competent technically as to raise the suspicion that art was their main occupation and the priestly life simply a means of support. The earliest was Mokuan, praised as the second Mu Ch'i, who went to China toward the middle of the fourteenth century and spent the last years of his life there. His paintings, a number of which were later imported to Japan, were so nearly like those of the Sung and Yüan masters that he was long thought

*Figure 25. Landscape. By Gaku-ô Zôkyû
(late fifteenth century).*

somewhat after the fashion in which the sculptors of the Heian and Kamakura periods had been honored. Much more renowned was the slightly later Josetsu, whose painting of a man trying to catch a fish with a gourd *(Plate 20)* was a treasured possession of the shogun Yoshimochi. Josetsu's gifted disciple Shûbun received for his artistic accomplishments an appointment as head of the painting bureau maintained by the shogunate. No fully authenticated work by him exists, but he was spoken of with extravagant praise by contemporary writers and regarded as a patriarch by most later members of the Chinese school. His style was probably similar to that of the late fifteenth century painter Gaku-ô Zôkyû *(Figure 25)*.

When we come to Sesshû, who lived from 1420 to 1506, there are many genuine paintings to prove that we are no longer dealing with a prototype or "early master." On the contrary, the works of this genius are the perfect aesthetic expression of the Zen spirit and the culmination of black-and-white art in Japan. Like Shûbun, Sesshû was a monk at the Shôkoku-ji, where he very likely received the guidance of his famous predecessor. He seems, however, to have been discontent with what he could learn in Japan, for in 1468 he went to China and studied for a year or more. He later said that he searched throughout the Middle Kingdom for a teacher, but found none worthy of his time save the mountains, rivers, rocks, and trees themselves. This is perhaps an injustice to the great Chinese artists of the day, but it helps explain the vitality of his Chinese landscapes. Not by any means realistic in the Western sense, they yet have an air of reality that could have come only from direct emotional experience.

Sesshû was the master of many styles. He himself distinguished three, which by analogy with calligraphy might be called cursive, semi-cursive, and non-cursive. The two landscapes shown here *(Plates 21 and 22)* illustrate the first and last categories. While the *haboku* painting is purely Chinese in conception and execution, the other is tempered by a delicacy of touch that is unmistakably Japanese in feeling. The same hint of softness is even more pronounced in some of Sesshû's other works, and for this reason he is credited with having begun the process whereby the Chinese monochrome was naturalized.

by the Japanese to have been a Chinese. A contemporary of Mokuan named Ka-ô, about whom virtually nothing is known, also left a number of expert paintings, of which the most appealing is an impressionistic sketch of the T'ang mystic Hanshan *(Plate 19)*.

In the early fifteenth century an artist called Minchô (1352–1431), or Chô Densu, exhibited such skill with the brush that he was given the rank of warden *(densu)* in a great monastery,

Sesshû's most prominent successors were Kanô Masanobu (1434–1530), Masanobu's son Motonobu (1466–1559), and Sesson (1504–1589?). Unlike the men mentioned hitherto, Masanobu was neither a priest nor a Zen devotee, but a professional painter. Although he studied under the monk Shûbun and worked on commission for Zen temples, he is known chiefly for having divorced Chinese-style painting from the Zen sect. The example shown here *(Plate 23),* which is one of his only two known works, appears to have been inspired by Chinese secular paintings of the Sung and Yüan periods. In 1467 Masanobu was appointed head of the shogun's bureau of painting, and for the succeeding four hundred years his family continued to enjoy official protection. As a result they became by far the most prosperous and influential, if not always the most creative, members of the artistic world.

The Kanô School, however, counted as its patriarch, not Masanobu, but Motonobu, whose works incorporate more of the traditional Japanese style than those of his father *(Figure 26).* Motonobu went so far as to employ coloring techniques borrowed from the *yamato-e,* but he was none the less an accomplished black-and-white draftsman, and the over-all framework of his paintings was Chinese. The Kanô family produced a number of other capable artists during the Muromachi period, but they are significant primarily as links between Motonobu and the great Momoyama representative of the clan, Eitoku, who is discussed below.

Sesson, who like Sesshû was a Zen priest, was perhaps closer to his great predecessor in spirit than the Kanô artists. Very little is known of him except that he lived out his life in his native district of Hitachi, which is in northeastern Japan. His work is rather uneven in quality, but the little painting shown here *(Plate 24)* is on a par with many of Sesshû's greater works.

As one might expect, in this age of the ink monochrome, the brilliant and colorful *yamato-e* fell into decline. Scrolls in the native style were produced, but they were as a rule conventionalized and spiritless. Among the artists that continued to work in this tradition, the most important belonged to the Tosa School, which was patronized by the emperor and the nobility. Tosa Mitsunobu (1434–1525), who was appointed chief painter to the imperial court in 1469, produced a number of works that seem to justify his honored position, but while expertly executed, they were essentially no more than pastiches composed of elements from earlier masterpieces. Nevertheless, they exerted a certain amount of influence on artists who had deserted the *yamato-e.* It is significant that Mitsunobu in his later years headed the shogun's bureau of painting, which was normally dominated by painters working in the Chinese manner.

Although Zen Buddhism gave new life to painting, its effect on sculpture was the opposite, for after all, this mystic faith eschewed the graven

Figure 26. Landscape. Kanô Motonobu.

image. Its monasteries were neither presided over by majestic golden Buddhas nor guarded by fiery demigods, and the detachment from the world that its adherents sought could hardly have been furthered by anything so tangible as a statue. At the same time, however, it would be an injustice to blame Zen alone with the deterioration of post-Kamakura sculpture. To be sure, it might have thrown sculptors out of work if it had entirely replaced the older forms of Buddhism, but this was not the case. The traditional sects continued to command a numerous following, and some even expanded. The trouble was that after the fourteenth century there were no consequential developments in Buddhist thought other than those associated with Zen. Old ideas were codified and reiterated, but one will search in vain for a fresh approach. The effect of this sterility on the arts was perhaps most disastrous in the case of sculpture, but it is also reflected in other fields as well. The eventual result was fortunately not a stifling of the arts, but simply an increased emphasis on their secular aspects.

Lack of imagination on the part of Buddhist artists did not always mean lack of taste. We may note for instance that the Muromachi period saw the construction of many fine Buddhist temples, among them quite a few of those that now create the celebrated "historical" atmosphere of Kyoto. Most of these buildings were eclectic in style, a good example being the main hall of the Kanshin-ji *(Plate 94)*. While this edifice is hardly what one would call exciting, its lines are good and its proportions sensible. The judicious combination of modes seen in its structural components was repeated with minor variations in countless later temples. The architects responsible for this copying might be collectively castigated for their want of originality, but they could easily have done worse.

While Buddhist architecture was thus becoming fixed, interesting changes were taking place in the construction of residences. A classic example until its destruction by fire in 1950 was the Kinkaku, or Golden Pavilion, built by Ashikaga Yoshimitsu around the turn of the fourteenth century. Of its three stories, the lower two followed the *shinden* style of the Heian period, while the uppermost was in the Chinese style *(kara-yô)* commonly employed for Zen monasteries. Somehow the two modes were in perfect harmony, and the whole

structure had a marvelous air of breezy elegance. It was a monument both to the luxurious life of the Ashikaga shoguns and to the restraint imposed by Zen aesthetics. The other famous sample of Muromachi residential architecture is the Ginkaku, or Silver Pavilion *(Plate 95),* erected by Yoshimitsu's grandson Yoshimasa as part of a mansion located in the suburbs of Kyoto. This building, which was obviously modeled on the Golden Pavilion, is not nearly so impressive, its chief importance lying in the fact that it incorporates many elements of the *shoin,* which was on the way to replacing the *shinden* as the typical dwelling of the upper classes. The *shoin* ("writing room") was originally a small study having a *tokonoma,* or alcove, and a window with a broad sill that could be used as a desk. It is thought to have appeared first in Zen monasteries and later to have been adopted into private houses. As it increased in importance, its name became attached to a type of dwelling of which it was a primary feature. Such buildings were usually partitioned into more sections than the *shinden* residence, and they were further distinguished by the use of sliding paper-covered doors and matted floors *(tatami),* which it will be observed are among the most notable accoutrements of the modern Japanese house.

Associated with the *shoin* was a new style of gardening, devised by Zen priests largely from Chinese models and aimed not at reproducing a famous scenic spot, as in the case of the *shinden* garden, but at expressing in succinct form the entire core and essence of nature. To this end trees and rocks were arranged in striking symbolic patterns, with emphasis on their mystic appeal. As is usual with Zen art, the keynote was economy. One very celebrated Muromachi garden still preserved, is nothing more than an abstract composition of curiously shaped rocks on immaculately swept white sand *(Plate 96)*. Its effect is not unlike that of a *haboku* landscape.

An exceedingly important cultural development of the Muromachi period was the perfection of the tea ceremonial. Tea had been introduced from China in early times, and during the Kamakura period had been prized as a beverage by Zen priests and members of the aristocracy, but the actual tea ritual does not seem to have gained favor until this era. Essentially it is no more than a small gathering of people who, while sipping tea and savoring the beauty of a work of art chosen for the occasion, engage in exceedingly polite conversation. The latter revolves about the art object on display, the beautiful bowls in which the tea is served, or a number of other aesthetic subjects, and its tone, like the preparing and drinking of the tea, is governed by strict rules, the preservation and teaching of which are prerogatives of the tea master. Devotees of the tea ceremony built special rooms or houses in which to perform it. In general, these were small and unobtrusive, but designed with fastidious regard for beauty of line and justness of proportion. In time they became the nucleus of a type of architecture that played an important role in the evolution of modern houses.

After the opening of trade with China, Chinese ceramic wares were highly valued as adjuncts to the tea ceremony, and their appearance inspired a revival of Japanese ceramics. Most active among the Japanese kilns were those of Seto, which began manufacturing a wide variety of wares modeled on Chinese patterns. Muromachi potters learned to produce delicate variations in glaze, and the technique for using the potter's wheel was greatly improved. Toward the end of the period Chinese-style ceramics were rivaled in popularity by unpretentious vessels of a type used in ordinary farm households. Almost always these contained flaws and distortions, but their rusticity appealed to

to followers of the *wabi* school of tea, who valued proximity to nature above all else.

Even the cast-iron kettles used by the tea masters were selected with a connoisseur's eye, those made in the districts of Ashiya and Sano being deemed the best. Ashiya kettles are comparatively refined in shape and smooth of surface *(Plate 82)*, while those of Sano are severely functional. On the whole, the metal craft reached a peak around the middle of the Muromachi period, and later pieces, aside from kettles, indicate a decline in imagination, if not in technical skill. Nevertheless, Japanese craftsmen never really lost the mastery of metal that had been displayed in the earliest historical periods *(Plate 83)*.

As a rule the cloth of this era was rather poor in quality. After the opening of trade with China, however, tea masters began to import satins, damasks, and other splendid Chinese fabrics, which they used for wrapping their tea utensils, and imitation of these materials led to an improvement in Japanese textiles.

Muromachi lacquer ware is distinguished by pictorial designs in the style of ink monochromes. At the same time, it shows a trend toward rusticity, with an accompanying loss of neatness and grace. It is a sign of the times that instead of the cosmetics kits used by great ladies in the previous eras, boxes for the ink stones of scholars are the most common relics *(Figure 27)*.

Figure 27. Two Ink-Stone Boxes. Maki-e. *Muromachi period.*

The influence of Zen Buddhism and the tea ceremony was evident in all the handiworks of this era. Emphasis was on simplicity, and there was a general avoidance of the bright colors so often found in Heian works. At the same time, the characteristic Japanese feeling for natural beauty was in prominence, especially in the utensils made toward the end of the period for use by the *wabi* school of the tea cult which flourished under the influence of Zen.

VII. THE MOMOYAMA PERIOD
1573 — 1615

During the last hundred years of the Muromachi period Japan was torn by feudal warfare accompanied by a general redistribution of property. By the opening of the sixteenth century the country had been divided into two or three hundred small districts under the control of autonomous military leaders. The local feudal systems had reached a state of relative stability, but there remained the task of binding them together under a central power. In the mid-sixteenth century Oda Nobunaga (1534–1582), a relatively unimportant landowner in the Owari district, began a series of military campaigns that were to end in national unity, though not until after his death. During the 1560's this brilliant warrior either defeated or made alliances with most of the minor feudatories, and in 1573 he extended his control over the Buddhist church, several branches of which had hitherto maintained formidable military establishments. Somewhat later he undertook to subdue the large landholders of the west and northeast, who were his only remaining opposition, but he died before this campaign was brought to completion.

Nobunaga's leading followers were Toyotomi Hideyoshi (1536–1598), a foot soldier who had risen from the ranks to become a general, and Tokugawa Ieyasu (1542–1616), a small vassal who had joined Nobunaga's forces after the defeat of his original lord. Nobunaga was succeeded by Hideyoshi, who brought the task of unification to completion. Not content with internal supremacy, however, the victorious commander in 1592 launched an invasion of Korea, with the ultimate object of conquering China. For a time his forces were successful, but by and by they bogged down on the Korean peninsula, and despite his sending reinforcements in 1597, little progress had been made when his death in 1598 brought an end to the experiment. The demise of Hideyoshi touched off a struggle for succession among his leading generals, ending in 1600 with the triumph of Tokugawa Ieyasu. In 1603 Ieyasu was appointed shogun, and although he was troubled for a few years afterward by recalcitrant supporters of Hideyoshi's son, the government that he established in the city of Edo was to be the longest lived and most powerful of the three great shogunates of feudal Japan.

Notwithstanding occasional battles between the great barons, the period after 1573 was for most of the country an era of peace. Industry and commerce thrived as never before, and they were further stimulated by the frequent arrival of traders from Europe, the first of whom had touched on Japanese shores in 1542. A new class of Japanese entrepreneurs appeared, and they joined the feudal lords, who were themselves mostly parvenus, in a merry search for pleasures and the finer things of life. The subtle, restrained tones sanctioned by Zen Buddhism and the canons of the tea ceremony had little attraction for these *nouveaux riches*. They preferred something big and dazzling. What they liked best was gold, and gold became the symbol of the era.

Nobunaga set the architectural tone for the period when in 1579 he built a huge castle at Azuchi, the main fortress of which was a towering seven-story structure with gleaming whitewashed walls. This was destroyed shortly after its construction, but several similar buildings are standing today, among which the most beautiful is that at Himeji *(Plate 97)*. The style of architecture displayed in this structure seems at a glance to owe something to Western influence, but Japanese authorities believe it to have developed from a form of watchtower used in Muromachi strongholds, though no doubt the need for citadels of its type arose from the introduction of Western firearms. Within the defenses of such fortresses there were spacious living apartments, constructed in a greatly magnified form of the *shoin* style. Like the donjons themselves, they contained huge galleries, the walls and doors of which painters of the age were called upon to decorate. New problems arose, since the traditional styles of painting were completely unsuited to these vast surfaces. The ink monochrome of the Muromachi period was too wanting in variety, while the polychromic *yamato-e* was too fragile. Rising to the occasion, Momoyama artists developed forms that combined the strong black contours of the one with the brilliant color of the other. Backgrounds were of glittering gold, and designs assumed heroic proportions.

In the late Muromachi period Kanô Motonobu had experimented with wall and screen paintings in a combination Chinese-and-Japanese style, and his son Hideyori (middle of the sixteenth century) had produced at least one work that belongs more to the new epoch than to the old *(Plate 25 and Figure 28)*, but the painter who deserves most credit for creating the Momoyama style was Motonobu's grandson Kanô Eitoku (1543–1590). Eitoku is recorded to have decorated the walls of Nobunaga's castle at Azuchi, but these no longer exist, and only a few paintings preserved in other places can be counted among his genuine works. The one shown here, which dates from his youth, lacks the gorgeous color that he employed during his later years, but it shows the daring brushwork and large-scale composition that form

the bonework of Momoyama painting *(Plate 27)*. Under Eitoku's leadership the Kanô School continued to hold the central position in the world of art. That it was able to do so was due largely to the patronage of Nobunaga and Hideyoshi, but the school nevertheless boasted a number of talented painters, of whom Eitoku's brother Naganobu (1577–1654) and his two sons, Mitsunobu and Takanobu, were the most famous. After the beginning of the Edo period, Kanô Sanraku (1559–1635) and Kanô Sansetsu (1586–1651) carried on the Momoyama tradition in Kyoto.

The Kanô School had no monopoly on the grandiose Momoyama style. On the contrary, a number of able rivals joined in the spirit of the new age, among whom we might mention particularly Kaihô Yûshô (1533–1615) and Hasegawa Tôhaku (1539–1610), each of whom left numerous magnificent screen and wall panels both in black and white and in color. Yûshô's ambition was to paint like the Sung master Liang K'ai, while Tôhaku admired Mu Ch'i. Direct reliance on Sung patterns gave the works of the two artists a freshness not often found among those of the Kanô School *(see Plate 28)*.

A somewhat different artist who also relied heavily on Liang K'ai and other Sung artists was the renowned swordsman Miyamoto Musashi (1584–1645), also known by the name Niten. Musashi left a number of paintings in a strongly individual style, all of which are in black and white. They vary in size from large screen panels to kakemonos such as the one shown here *(Plate 29)*. All display the powerful brushwork associated

Figure 28. Maple-Viewers at Mt. Takao. Kanô Hideyori.

with the Momoyama period, but they defy any attempt to classify them in any one school.

The condition of the Tosa School in this period is indicated by the fact that Tosa Mitsuyoshi, one of its leading members, was reduced to drawing drafts and underpaintings for Kanô artists. The languishing tradition of the *yamato-e,* however, was rescued at about this time by Tawaraya Sôtatsu, who used it as the basis for a new art. Virtually nothing is known about Sôtatsu except that he was a friend of a famous connoisseur named Hon'ami Kôetsu, who led a little coterie of artists bound together by a devotion to the tea ceremony and similar pursuits. More or less under the tutelage of Kôetsu, Sôtatsu developed a very original style in which line, ordinarily the most fundamental element of Japanese painting, was subordinated to color. He achieved the subtlest variations in shading by retouching the original coloring while still wet. His screen paintings *(Plate 30 and Figure 29)* were frequently based on literary classics, but unlike the usual *yamato-e,* they made no attempt to tell a story, the emphasis being instead upon decorative effect.

Momoyama textiles and lacquer ware show the same brilliance as painting. By this time the ordinary costume for men and women alike was the simple kimono. The fashion was to divide the surface design into distinct compartments. A typical kimono of the age might have a flowered cloth around the shoulders and the foot, with a plain white fabric in the middle. Sometimes the garment

was divided in half vertically with different fabrics on each side, or composed of contrasting cloths sewn together in large alternating squares. The embroidery of the era is especially remarkable. Colorful hand-sewn fabrics like that reproduced here *(Plate 76)* were made more dazzling by liberal applications of gold and silver foil. The lacquer wares of the age are also marked by a lavish use of the precious metals. At the same time, however, there was a revival of the lacquer painting, which, though not perhaps so flashy as the golden *maki-e,* satisfied the current demand for color *(Plate 80).*

Ceramic wares continued to show the strong influence of the tea ceremony. By this time Chinese styles had almost been entirely displaced by those of the native kilns. The Seto potters were especially noted for their yellow and black tea bowls, while vessels from the Iga area were prized for their artlessness *(Plate 68).* Among the many other types of ware, mention might be made of Oribe *(Plate 66),* which takes its name from that of the tea master Furuta Oribe Masashige, and *raku (Plate 67),* which is named after a mansion built by Hideyoshi. The invasion of Korea (1592–1598) led to the introduction of Korean pottery, and this was imitated in many localities. Korean porcelain, imported at the same time, served as models from which the craftsmen of the Edo period developed the beautiful Japanese color glazes now famous everywhere.

No outline of the Momoyama period could be

Figure 29. Ancient Dance. Sôtatsu.

Figure 30. Lacquered Container for the Host. Momoyama period.

ended without reference to the many works that were inspired by contact with Europe. Aside from imitating Western art, Japanese artists attempted to adapt Western motifs to native forms like the screen painting *(Plate 31)* and the *maki-e (Figure 30)*. The results are usually incongruous and some-times crude, but they show an urge on the part of Japanese artists to enrich their heritage with new ideas and methods. Though Western subject matter was as a whole discarded in the Edo period, certain artists continued to experiment with West-ern shading and perspective.

VIII. THE EDO PERIOD
1615 — 1867

In the realm of art, the transition from the Momoyama to the Edo period was so gradual that to set a date at which one ended and the other began is even more artificial than usual. At the same time, it is necessary somehow to distinguish the two periods, since the styles most characteristic of them are quite different. The dividing line chosen here, 1615, is the year in which Tokugawa Ieyasu conquered the last of Hideyoshi's supporters and effectively brought the entire country under his rule. This date, however, is selected not be-cause of its political significance but because it falls toward the pivot of the long transition. The administrative and social institutions that charac-terized Japan under Tokugawa rule had not yet crystallized, but the general tone of the epoch to follow had been set. For one thing, the program of political and economic expansion initiated by

Hideyoshi had largely been abandoned, and the first steps had been taken toward expelling the foreign influences hitherto tolerated in pursuance of his plans. To be sure, the notorious Tokugawa policy of isolation was not yet in effect, but it was reasonably clear that the new shogunate had no intention of allowing foreign relations to inter-fere with its control of the nation. Internally, while there was still a certain amount of fluidity in society, stratification had already set in to a con-siderable extent. In brief, the state had not yet decided, as it ultimately did decide, to attempt to maintain the status quo forever, but it was beginning to see that its own fate rested on its ability to resist rapid change. The spirit of the times was definitely conservative, and it exercised as much restraint on the arts as on any other aspect of life.

Architecture continued to be very much as it had been during the Momoyama period. The general lines of castles and temples hardly varied at all, although there was a trend toward less boldness and more decorative finery. The celebrated Tôshô-gû at Nikko will serve as an illustration. Built as a mausoleum for Ieyasu by his son and grandson, this shrine was evidently intended to be the ultimate in magnificence. Artists and carpenters were summoned from all over the country to participate in its construction, and the most expensive materials were used unstintingly. The finished buildings, however, while following patterns set in the Momoyama period, fail utterly to match the grandeur achieved in that age, the only stylistic innovation of note being the addition of a vast amount of ornamentation that can only be described as rococo. The colors are bright, and admirable craftsmanship is displayed in the ubiquitous gewgaws, but there is a sore lack of inspiration, and it might be said, of taste. The gaudy decorations in Momoyama palaces were in many ways subject to the same criticism, but they were at once more imaginative and better in agreement with the whole design. In the Edo period there was a strong tendency toward irrelevant display of technique—in short, toward meaningless frills.

Outstanding exceptions are found in the Katsura Palace *(Plates 98, 99, and 100)*, the Shugaku-in, and other buildings that were products of the tea ceremony tradition. These modest structures are completely free of unnecessary trimmings. Made of unfinished logs, bamboo stalks, straw, and earth, they seem almost to have grown by themselves out of their natural surroundings. Their simplicity, like that of the tea ceremony itself, was no doubt painstakingly contrived, but that does not rob them of their lasting beauty. Embodied in these cottages are the canons of taste that have lately won worldwide acclaim for Japanese residential architecture.

One of the phenomena that most influenced art during the Edo period was the advance in status of commoners. Hitherto, Japanese art had been produced almost exclusively for the nobility or the warriors, but now there came into existence a sizable group of merchants and artisans financially able to act as patrons, and in response to their desires, artists of the period created vivacious new forms. In contrast, the increasingly conservative art produced for the upper classes seems faded and lifeless. It points up the intellectual sterility that prevailed in the highest places.

As in the previous age, the Kanô School was dominant in the world of painting. Kanô Tan'yû (1602–1674) moved from his ancestral home in Kyoto to Edo in 1617, in order to work for the shogunate, and four years later he was made head of the official bureau of painting. An artist of great diligence, Tan'yû not only studied and copied innumerable masterpieces by earlier Chinese and Japanese artists, but also turned out a large collection of original works *(Plate 32)*. Many of his sketches are quite lively and imaginative, but his larger paintings are disappointingly shackled

Figure 31. Tiger. Kanô Naonobu.

by tradition. Nevertheless he was the master of a sound style, and he was widely imitated by later artists. His younger brother Naonobu (1607–1650), who was also patronized by the Tokugawas, was in some respects his equal *(Figure 31)*. Unfortunately, however, Naonobu died before reaching maturity. After the passing of these two men, Kanô artists did little more than transmit the techniques they had inherited. They were, however, exceedingly in demand. In addition to serving the shogunate, they were employed by a good number of the provincial lords, and their prestige, as well as their family organization, spread throughout the nation. Unhappily, their comfortable social and financial situation seems to have dampened their artistic urge, or at least their will to create anything new. It should be noted, however, that after the collapse of the Tokugawas it was Kanô Hôgai and Hashimoto Gahô, both members of this ancient school, who carried the principles of traditional Japanese art into modern times.

Virtually nothing of interest in the form of the traditional *yamato-e* was produced during this era. The Tosa School was for a time given new life by the adoption of certain Chinese elements, but its decline was not long interrupted. Toward the last of the Edo period there occurred in connection with the nationalist political movement a revival of the Heian *yamato-e*, but although it showed some promise for a time, it was short-lived. On the other hand, the school founded by Sôtatsu, which owed a great deal to the Heian scroll paintings, produced a number of noteworthy artists. The most gifted was Ogata Kôrin (1658–1716), who carried the style of Sôtatsu to new heights. Born the son of a rich merchant, Kôrin was also a distant kinsman of Hon'ami Kôetsu, and, like Kôetsu, a man of great parts. Aside from painting, he made expert lacquer ware and drew designs for pottery and clothing. Shown here are one of his most brilliant screen paintings *(Plate 33)* and a lacquer box with a similar pattern *(Plate 81)*. Kôrin had a number of well-known followers, but the true successor to his art was Sakai Hôitsu (1761–1828), a man of noble birth who renounced his station in order to devote his life to art and literature. Having studied the styles of the Kanô, Tosa, and Shijô Schools, he eventually settled on that of Kôrin. His masterpiece is a painting of summer and autumn plants *(Plate 34)*. A purely ornamental work, it nevertheless reveals an admirable sense of natural form.

The Tokugawa government, while attempting to shut out all influence from the West, was not indiscriminately anti-foreign. On the contrary, it actively fostered the study of China and particularly of Confucianism, in which it no doubt saw a philosophical support for its conservative policies. One unforeseen result was that many of the educated men of the time came under the influence of Ming and Ch'ing gentleman-scholars, and like them turned to art as a means of free expression. During the Ming period in China the paintings of the government-sponsored academy had become harsh and frigid for want of originality. Technically impeccable, they yet lacked the spark of inspiration that might have made them vital and moving. In revolt against this sterile art, and vaguely against the authority that supported it, a group of scholars in southern China had developed a new style of painting that was somewhat amateurish in technique, but genuine and amiable in spirit. This came to be called the "Southern-Painting" style, or in Japanese *nanga*, in contrast to the "Northern-Painting" style associated with the academy. Like the Ming government the Tokugawa shogunate was dedicated to the suppression of new ideas, and the art that it fostered was as a result staid and repetitive. The Japanese Confucianists of the Edo period were, therefore, in circumstances that resembled those of the Ming scholars, and it is hardly surprising that they received the Chinese *nanga* style with enthusiasm.

The most famous of the Japanese scholar-painters were Yosa Buson (1717–1783) and Ike no Taiga (1723–1776). Both painted in a very free and candid manner, but Taiga was the more original. The example of his work shown here *(Plate 35)*, which is from a series of paintings made in cooperation with Buson, clearly illustrates the unrestrained, lyric approach that typifies the Japanese *nanga*. Among the later artists of this group, Uragami Gyokudô (1745–1820), Aoki Mokubei (1775–1833) *(Plate 36)*, Tanomura Chikuden (1777–1837), Tani Bunchô (1763–1840), and Watanabe Kazan (1793–1841) are conspicuous. There were innumerable others, working in a profusion of styles, but they shared in common a strong urge toward individualism—they were concerned first and foremost with ex-

Figure 32. Sketches from Nature. Maruyama Ôkyo.

pressing their own feelings. Art to them was, after all, a means of personal escape from the boredom of a rigidly regulated society. As a result, their paintings were a relief from the works of the Kanô School, but at the same time they sometimes failed for the lack of sufficient technical skill.

Allowances made for the age-old idealism of Oriental art, the painting of the Edo period was surprisingly realistic. Even Tan'yû, the formalist, and Kôrin, the champion of the ornamental, made countless faithful sketches from nature as a foundation for their styles. A closer approach to realism, however, is found in the works of Maruyama Ôkyo (1733–1795) and his disciples. Ôkyo as a youth studied the Kanô tradition, but having become discontent with its archaic methods, set out to find a new style that would enable him to show the beauty of nature as it actually appeared. He was aided in his search by the discovery of Western perspective, displayed in imported Dutch etchings. Despite his efforts, however, Ôkyo did not completely escape the bonds of idealism, and his works are perhaps best described as naturalistic rather than realistic *(Figure 32)*. The Maruyama-Shijô School, which he founded, is noted for its accurate, though somewhat sentimental, treatment of natural objects. Unfortunately, the foundations for its realism were weak, and the works of its members often have that banal quality seen in twentieth-century imitations of Western art.

The Sôtatsu-Kôrin, Nanga, and Maruyama-Shijô Schools all enjoyed a certain amount of popularity, but what pleased the ordinary town-dweller most was a new class of genre pictures that dealt with subjects familiar to him. These were rooted in Momoyama representations of people at work or at play *(Plates 25 and 26)*. The Momoyama examples, however, were as a rule painted on screens and sliding doors for the houses of the rich, and they were based primarily on the life of the upper classes. The new paintings took their inspiration and their subjects instead from the theater, the gay quarters, the restaurants, the wrestling arenas, and the other centers of ephemeral pleasure in Edo. These places, with their retinues of actors, courtesans, merchants, dissolute samurai, and such like, constituted what was known appropriately as the "floating world" *(ukiyo),* and pictures of life in this demimonde were called "pictures of the floating world," or *ukiyo-e.* It was these rather than the more subdued and tasteful works of traditional artists that captured the imagination of the common man in the city.

An art for the masses, however, required not only new subject matter, but a means of gaining wide circulation. This problem was solved in the middle decades of the seventeenth century by a painter named Hishikawa Moronobu *(Plate 37),* who hit upon the idea of printing his pictures with wood blocks. Thereafter *ukiyo-e* became both plentiful and cheap, and during the succeeding century alone millions of them, mostly pictures of actors or beautiful women, were produced. In this interval numerous artists were idolized by the general populace, the most famous being the "three Toriis," Kiyonobu (1664–1729), Kiyomasu (early eighteenth century), and Kiyomitsu (1735–1785). No great new developments occurred, however, until Suzuki Harunobu (1725–1770) published his first prints in a new colorful style in 1765. Hitherto, aside from the black outlines, red and green had been the only two colors used, but Harunobu invented a method for printing more than ten. At the same time, he introduced more complex subjects than had so far been the rule *(Plate 38)*. His beautiful love scenes, with their incredibly graceful human figures and detailed settings, made his pictures so popular that the last few years of his life are called the "Harunobu period" in the history of the *ukiyo-e*.

Torii Kiyonaga (1752–1815) adopted much from Harunobu, but changed his doll-like heroines into healthy grown-up women *(Figure 33)*, and Kitagawa Utamaro (1756–1803), who followed Kiyonaga, was even more successful in conveying the sensual elements in feminine beauty *(Plate 39)*. A number of other artists of the day concentrated on the faces of actors instead of women. Of these, none excelled Tôshûsai Sharaku, who, during a short period of activity in the years 1794 and 1795, produced some of the most powerful and individual *ukiyo-e* of all *(Plate 40)*.

There was a limit, however, to what could be done with the subjects that were being handled, and after the Kansei era (1789–1800) there was obviously need for a new approach. Fortunately, about this time Katsushika Hokusai (1760–1849), inspired to some extent by Dutch etchings, began to produce landscapes in the *ukiyo-e* style, taking as a rule subjects familiar to the residents of Edo. His best and most famous work is a set of prints showing Mt. Fuji from many different points of view *(Plate 41)*.

Hokusai was succeeded by Andô Hiroshige (1797–1858), who employed similar subjects, but treated them in a more romantic style *(Plate 43)*. After these two great landscape artists, the *ukiyo-e* passed almost into oblivion in Japan. It was "discovered" by French artists, however, in about 1855, and it later exerted a significant influence on Degas, Manet, Cézanne, Van Gogh, and many

other impressionists of the nineteenth century.

During the Edo period the traditional crafts reached new peaks of perfection, but subsequently fell victim to the same technical over-refinement as is seen in architecture and painting. The main trend in the field of ceramics was a shift from pottery to porcelain. The Korean technique for making porcelain with simple underglaze designs was imported in the course of Hideyoshi's Korean wars and used in the early seventeenth century at a number of kilns in Kyushu. Somewhat later a potter named Sakaida Kakiemon, who worked at the Arita kiln in what is now Saga Prefecture, developed an overglaze technique for making polychromic designs, which rapidly spread to the other provinces. Kakiemon was so widely imitated that it is impossible to distinguish his works from many by other artists, and his name is applied generally to pieces done in his style *(Plate 69)*. The porcelain produced in the Arita area as a whole is known as Imari ware *(Plate 70)*, after the name of the trading center where it was

Figure 33. A Cool Evening. Torii Kiyonaga.

marketed. In the seventeenth century, Kakiemon and Imari porcelain vessels were carried by the Dutch to Europe, where they were highly appreciated by lovers of *chinoiserie* and even copied by a number of potters.

Kakiemon's technique was adopted by the somewhat later Kyoto ceramist Ninsei, who made his wares more colorful by adding gold and silver. His designs, which are characteristically Japanese, call to mind the lavish screen paintings of the Momoyama period. The jar shown here *(Plate 72)*, for example, has a pattern of cherry blossoms that might equally well have been used by an Eitoku for a castle wall painting.

One of the most important types of porcelain that developed from Kakiemon's style was Kutani. According to a legend, the lord of Kaga Province, which is now Ishikawa Prefecture, sent a vassal to Arita to learn Kakiemon's technique, and the latter upon his return set up a kiln in the town of Kutani, which gave its name to this ware. The first period of activity there did not last beyond the seventeenth century, but the kiln again began producing in the nineteenth century, and Kutani products are still popular today. The early pieces are called "Old Kutani" to distinguish them from those of modern times. Old Kutani was made with both pictorial and abstract designs in

Figure 34. Nabeshima Porcelain. Edo period.

deep red, blue, green, yellow, and purple *(Plate 71)*.

By the end of the seventeenth century, the large-scale Momoyama patterns had been completely replaced by smaller and more elaborate designs. At the same time, the florid styles of Ch'ing China were being imitated at some kilns. These latter are more or less evident in Nabeshima porcelain *(Figure 34)*, which was perfected during the early eighteenth century, and which represents a pinnacle of technical mastery.

With the popularization of tea drinking, the demand for ceramic products increased, but mass production brought about a decline in quality. Still, in Kyoto the best traditions were kept alive, and in the early nineteenth century some of the most beautiful of all Japanese porcelain wares were turned out there. They include many varieties, but few of the pieces are lovelier than the bowl by Nin'ami Dôhachi (1784–1855) reproduced here *(Plate 73)*.

During the latter part of the Edo period the ceramic arts spread into many outlying provinces, some of which became and have remained famous for their wares. As a rule, the local products are based on one or another of the types mentioned above, but they show many interesting innovations and variations.

The textile arts underwent a brilliant development in the Edo period. Designs on kimonos

Figure 35. Kimono with Yûzen Pattern. Edo period.

finally broke through the compartments of earlier times and spread over the entire surface. Often they were executed in embroidery and metal foil, as previously, but new techniques enabled craftsmen to achieve much the same effect with woven or dyed patterns. From China there came a method for making a luxurious fabric known as *karaori*, which is marked by spendthrift use of gold and silver thread. Many kimonos made of this material appear at first glance to have been embroidered *(Plate 77)*. It was produced primarily in the Nishijin District of Kyoto, destined later to become the most famous Japanese textile center. This era also witnessed the development of the Yûzen process of dyeing, which allowed for the creation of designs even freer and more colorful than those that could be made by embroidery *(Figure 35)*. Perhaps even more important than these technical improvements, however, was the spread of the textile industry to the provincial areas. Almost all of the renowned local Japanese silks of the present day are produced in factories that originated in these times.

Lacquer ware tended to become cluttered with flawlessly executed, but artistically meaningless, details. However, a number of beautiful pieces were produced by individual artists, such as Igarashi Dôho, Ogawa Haritsu, and Ogata Kôrin *(Plate 81)*. Moreover, as in the case of textiles, the production of lacquer was carried to outlying areas, where numerous original styles were created. Many of the provincial manufactures survived the Meiji Restoration of 1868 and have made a place for themselves in modern industry.

IX. CONCLUSION

The history of Japan until the late nineteenth century is, in a sense, the history of the spread of Chinese civilization to the Japanese islands and, no less important, of the reaction it called forth from the Japanese. It is probably no exaggeration to say that in every phase of life the latter have at some time or another been influenced by their affluent neighbors, but the process whereby the culture of a great continental nation was adopted into a small insular kingdom was, of necessity, not simply a matter of sheer copying. On the contrary, since what was suitable and pleasing to the Chinese was usually somewhat unnatural and frequently totally alien to the islanders, the imported cultural elements were almost invariably reinterpreted, revised, or altogether rejected. The result was the formation of a Japanese culture which, while rooted in Chinese civilization, was nevertheless an entity in itself.

The influence of China is as evident in art as anywhere else, but the mature arts of Japan contrast greatly with those of China. Differences in physical environment and in aesthetic sense between the Japanese and Chinese caused them to seek and to find different modes of expression. The ordinary pattern in the historical development of Japanese art began with simple imitation of an imported object or form. At first the copywork was faithful, even slavish, but presently someone decided that a few changes would help. The alterations went on and on, until finally there was little or nothing left of the original. The striking feature of this process is that, whatever the field of art, the changes reveal a general trend toward softness, intimacy, and liveliness. This is so pronounced that it cannot be explained as accidental, and one can only conclude that it comes from something basic in the Japanese psyche —something that rejects much of the dignity and austerity that characterize Chinese art in favor of a warmer, more natural, type of beauty. If the present volume helps the reader to see and understand this fundamental Japanese attitude, it will have attained its goal.

PART TWO   PLATES

WALL PAINTING *(detail)*
330×260 cm. Formerly in the Hôryû-ji, Nara Prefecture.

The priceless murals in the main sanctuary, or "Golden Hall," of the Hôryû-ji *(Plate 85)* were nearly destroyed in the fire that gutted that building in 1949. There had been twelve panels of murals, four wide and eight narrow. On each of the wide panels was depicted the paradise of a Buddha, while on each of the narrow ones there appeared a single standing Bodhisattva. There is no documentary proof concerning the date of the paintings, but it can be assumed without the likelihood of great error that they were produced at about the same time as a group of clay statues in the five-storied pagoda *(Plate 86)* at the same monastery, which are dated Wadô 4, or 711. There is an early record to the effect that the murals were painted by a Korean named Donchô, who immigrated to Japan in 610, but this tradition has been so thoroughly disproven that we need not refute it here.

Several theories exist as to the identity of the four paradise scenes on the larger panels, but they all agree that the western panel displayed the paradise of Amida. A detail from this is shown here. The walls themselves were about six inches thick and were entirely covered with *kaolin*. With this as a background, the paintings were executed in coloring so thick that it remained bright and clear in many places until the fire of 1949. The beautiful faces and graceful bodies of the Buddhas and Bodhisattvas in these paintings are features akin to the style of Buddhist murals in India, but they no doubt entered Japan by way of China rather than directly.

48

PLATE 2   PAINTING

NARA PERIOD [645—794]

SCREEN PORTRAIT OF A WOMAN *(detail)*
In color on paper. 126×66 cm.   Owner: Shôsô-in, Nara Prefecture.

In 756, on the occasion of a ceremony commemorating the seventh week after the death of the Emperor Shômu, the widowed Empress Kômyô presented her deceased husband's personal belongings to the Great Buddha at the Tôdaiji. Among these articles, which today make up the principal holdings of the Shôsô-in Repository, is found the present screen portrait. Originally, the clothing of the lady shown in the painting consisted of bird feathers attached to the canvas, but these have fallen off, and now only the underpainting remains Dresses decorated with feathers were fashionable among upper-class Chinese ladies during the reign of the Emperor Chung Tsung of T'ang (684–705, 709), and the present portrait is doubtless from about that time. There is some color—the face of the lady is tinted slightly, and her lips are painted red—but the treatment of line is typical of ink monochromes in this epoch.

50

PLATE 3   PAINTING

NARA PERIOD [645—794]

Kichijô-ten (Mahasri) *(detail)*
*In color on hemp cloth.   54.2×32.0 cm.   Owner: Yakushi-ji, Nara
Prefecture.*

Kichijô-ten is a benevolent goddess who bestows money and other
material benefits on her worshipers. Her cult was strong in Japan
during the late Nara period, and images of her were produced both
as icons and as *objets d'art*. Among the many likenesses of her that
have been preserved, this one from the Yakushi-ji is particularly
renowned. Executed in color on fine hemp cloth, it is only 54.2 by
32.0 centimeters in size, but it gives the impression of being quite
large. The goddess appears to be walking quietly toward the left.
Her hair is adorned with a jeweled headdress, as is ordinary with
Buddhist figures, and in her hand she holds a *hôshu,* or sacred jewel,
which according to Buddhist lore brings to its possessor many
miraculous powers. Her raiment, however, is the usual ceremonial
dress of Nara period ladies, and if it were not for the sacred gem,
the headdress, and the halo, she would impress one as being not
a deity, but simply a beautiful woman. Indeed, her plump cheeks,
her brightly-painted lips, and her long thin eyes have an altogether
sensual appearance. This image bears a strong resemblance to certain
portraits excavated in Central Asia, as well as to the screen portrait
shown in the previous plate, and we may well assume that all of
these paintings represented a Chinese ideal of feminine beauty that
had spread to surrounding territories.

52

PLATE 4   PAINTING

HEIAN PERIOD [794—1185]

IMAGE OF FUDÔ MYÔ-Ô (ACALANATHA) *(detail)*
In color on silk.   164.8×95.7 cm.   Owner: Myô-ô-in, Wakayama
Prefecture.

This painting is known as the "Red Fudô" of Mt. Kôya. According to tradition, Chishô Daishi, a great priest of the Japanese Tendai sect, once saw the deity Fudô in a vision and later had the apparition drawn in blood taken from his own head, the result being this image. Thanks to this legend, the work is classed in a category of imaginative works known as "vision pictures." Fudô sits on a great boulder, one knee bent horizontally. In his right hand he holds a sword, around which is coiled a dragon, and in his left a rope, both the sword and the rope being the usual symbols of his power. He has two attendants, both of whom are, contrary to the usual pattern, placed on the same side of him.   Because of this odd arrangement and of certain unique features in the drafting, opinions vary concerning the date of this work.   Some scholars hold it to be from the very first of the Heian period, but others place it at the end of that period or even as late as the Kamakura period. The truth probably lies somewhere between these extremes.

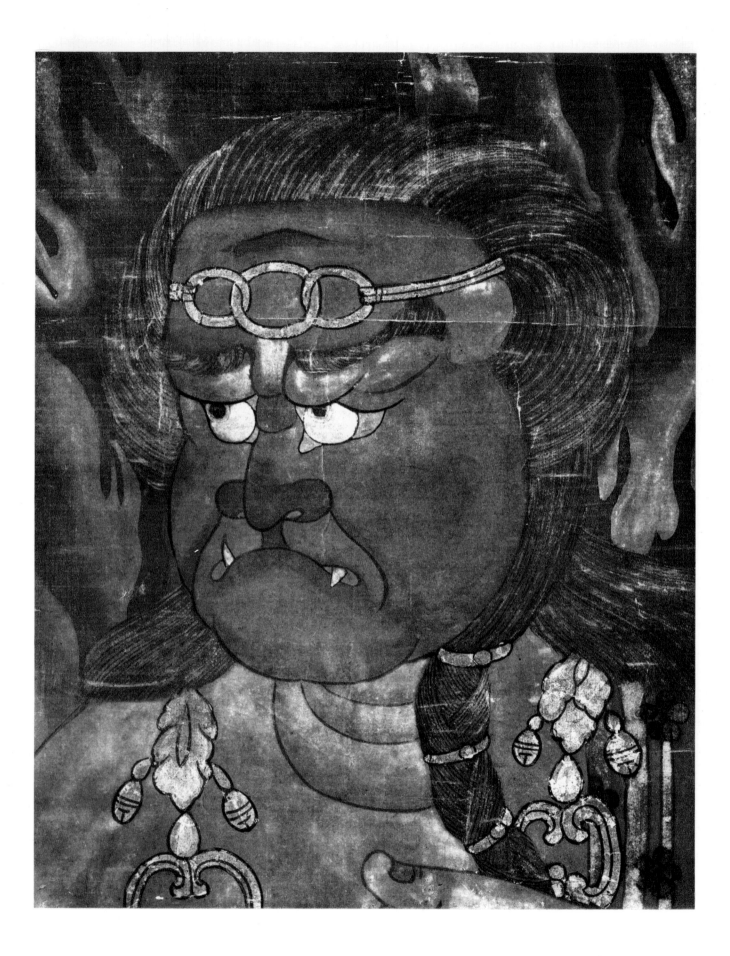

PLATE 5 PAINTING

HEIAN PERIOD [794—1185]

IMAGE OF KUJAKU MYÔ-ô (MAHAMAYURI)
In color on silk. 148.7×98.9 cm.. Owner: The Hara Collection, Kanagawa Prefecture.

The present painting is in the classic form of Heian pictorial icons. The "Enlightened King" Kujaku (Mahamayuri) is shown full-face, and the painted surface is almost completely filled up by the deity and the peacock on which he is seated. In later periods, the subject was usually smaller in relation to the surface and was frequently shown in half-profile. Ordinarily, divinities of the "Enlightened King" category are portrayed in fierce aspects, but Kujaku is an exception. He invariably appears as a benevolent and compassionate being, for, just as the peacock eats poisonous plants and noxious insects, Kujaku, whose name means "peacock," is thought to consume the passion, anger, and ignorance that infect the human mind. He usually has four arms, as in the present case, but there are instances in which he is shown with two or six. His cult was strong toward the end of the Heian period, and this image is probably a product of that era. The contours of his body are in red, and those of his clothing in black Chinese ink. Within these outlines brilliant color has been applied, with cut-gold ornamentation here and there. Aside from being a fine specimen of late Heian Buddhist art, this work is one of the most outstanding paintings of its day.

PLATE 6   PAINTING

HEIAN PERIOD [794—1185]

IMAGE OF THE BODHISATTVA FUGEN (SAMANTABHADRA)
In color on silk.   159.4×74.5 cm.   Owner: Tokyo National Museum.

Fugen is thought by Buddhists to be the protector of the *Lotus Sutra*
and its believers, and his cult spread together with the Tendai sect,
which regarded this sutra as its principal canonical text. Several late
Heian images of him have come down to the present time. Among
them, the one shown here is the most beautiful, and, indeed, it is
one of the greatest masterpieces of Heian painting. The Bodhisattva
sits on a white six-tusked elephant. With his eyes cast somewhat
downward and his palms held together in a holy gesture, he seems
surrounded by an aura of peace. Theoretically, Bodhisattvas are
neither male nor female, and although Fugen most commonly
appears as the former this image rather suggests a very beautiful
woman. At the same time there is an air of holiness about it. In effect,
the artist, while painting a graceful ideal of womanhood managed to
permeate his work with religious feeling. The painting is through
and through a product of late Heian delicacy.

58

PLATE 7   SCROLL PAINTING

HEIAN PERIOD [794—1185]

THE TALE OF GENJI *(detail from the section entitled "Azuma-ya")*
Three paper scrolls in color. Section: 21.4×47.9 cm. Owner: Reimei-
kai, Tokyo.

This work is no longer in scroll form, but has been cut into sections,
which are now mounted individually. One hesitates to say definitely
how many scrolls the series originally comprised, but, to judge from
the content of the existing sections, about ten must have been required
to cover the fifty-four chapters of the *Tale of Genji.* The famous
novel, written by Lady Murasaki during the early eleventh century,
is not given in complete form; rather, from one to three excerpts
from each chapter are presented with accompanying illustrations,
the quotations alternating with the paintings. The latter are "still
pictures," which agree almost to the letter with the texts on which
they are based, and it is evident that at this early stage in the
development of picture scrolls the pictorial parts were completely
ancillary to the written portions.

The Genji scrolls have long been attributed to the painter Fujiwara
Takayoshi, who was active during the first half of the twelfth century.
Although the attribution is open to question, it is probably not a mistake to date the work at about the time of Takayoshi. It is possible
that the paintings were done by several artists, instead of only one.

The lavish colors and quiet lines create an atmosphere of beauty
and opulence that accords well with the aesthetic outlook of the
Heian patricians. The narrow slits for eyes and simple hooks for
noses make the characters singularly expressionless, and somehow
convey to the viewer a feeling of loneliness. Could it be that these
faces were intended to express the "sadness of things" spoken of so
often by Heian writers? In typical *yamato-e* fashion, the roofs of the
houses have been omitted so that the interiors, which fill most of the
space, can be seen. The people as well as the furnishings in the rooms
are proportionately larger than the buildings. The point from which
the scene is viewed is in each case above and at an angle. Paintings
which incorporate the features here outlined are known as *tsukuri-e*
(a term which originally signified a painting in which the contours
were drawn first and the color added later). They form one of the
main sub-types of the *yamato-e.*

60

PLATE 8   PAINTING

HEIAN PERIOD [794—1185]

PAINTING ON A SUTRA SCROLL *(detail)*
*In color on paper. Height: 26.3 cm. Owner: The Itsukushima Shrine,
Hiroshima Prefecture.*

There is preserved in the Itsukushima Shrine a collection of thirty-
three scrolls supposed to have been donated in 1164 by the great
Chancellor Taira no Kiyomori (1118–1181) and his family. Of the
thirty-three, twenty-eight are devoted to a copy of the *Lotus Sutra,*
and each of four others contains a short sutra, while the remaining
one bears a dedication ostensibly written by Kiyomori. Each of the
scrolls is decorated differently. The paper bindings, handles, metal
fittings, and boxes, are all the ultimate in elegance, and at the
beginning of each scroll there is a painting in *yamato-e* style. Some
of the pictures more or less faithfully illustrate the contents of the
scrolls to which they are appended, while others show people paying
ceremonial tribute to the *Lotus Sutra,* and still others consist of
pattern-like birds and flowers that give symbolic form to the teachings
of that scripture. The present work is of the second type. It shows
a priest seated in his mountain hut and chanting the sutra.

These scrolls have traditionally been said to have been written by
thirty-two members of the house of Taira, but modern research
indicates that this story of their provenance is a fabrication. In the
first place, only three signatures aside from Kiyomori's appear, and
those are of relatively minor members of the Taira clan, namely
Morikuni, Shigeyasu, and Morinobu. Furthermore, the signature of
Kiyomori looks very much like a forgery by Shigeyasu, and the sutra
texts as a whole appear to have been drafted by two or three professional sutra-copyists, rather than by thirty-two individuals. All in
all, it seems unlikely that any of the Taira other than the three
persons whose names are authentically signed had anything to do
with the donation of the sutras.

62

PLATE 9   SCROLL PAINTING

HEIAN PERIOD [794—1185]

THE HISTORY OF MT. SHIGI *(detail)*
From the second of three paper scrolls in color.   31.5×1274 cm.
Owner: Chôgo Sonshi-ji, Nara Prefecture.

The three scrolls of the present work depict miraculous stories about
a monk named Myôren and his elder sister, who was a nun. Myôren
lived in the Chôgo Sonshi-ji, a monastery on Mt. Shigi, the principal
deity of which was Bishamon-ten (Vaisravana). The first scroll in
the series tells of Myôren's having caused a rice granary to take flight
by performing ceremonies before this god. The second deals with
a tradition according to which the monk once cured the Emperor
Daigo (reigned 898–930) of an illness by appealing to the same
deity. The final scroll recounts how Myôren's sister set out to look
for him and, after much searching, had the direction pointed out
for her by the Great Buddha at Nara. Each of the scrolls has unique
stylistic features, but they are all relatively light in coloring, the
emphasis being on movement. The mode of expression as a whole
is in complete contrast to the quietness of the *Tale of Genji* scrolls.
The artist has, by making full use of flowing ink lines, endowed
the work with amazing vitality. According to tradition, the Archbishop Kakuyû (1053–1140) was the painter, but there is no proof
for this attribution. In any event, the scrolls were probably painted
by a first-rate artist of the late Heian period.

The scene shown, which is from the story about the faith-healing
of the Emperor Daigo, shows a child attendant of Bishamon-ten
flying down from heaven on a cloud. His hair and clothing, as well
as the lances he is carrying, trail behind him in the wind, and a wheel
symbolizing the Buddha's power rolls before him. In the dynamic
treatment of these elements can be seen the most important single
trait of this work—speed.

64

PLATE 10 SCROLL PAINTING

HEIAN PERIOD [794—1185]

FROLIC OF THE ANIMALS *(detail)*
From the first of four paper scrolls in black and white. 30.9×1148.4 cm.
Owner: Kôzan-ji, Kyoto.

The title of the present work is somewhat misleading, since actually
only the first two scrolls and part of the third are animal caricatures,
the remaining portions being devoted to comic representations of
people. The first scroll shows frogs, monkeys, and hares behaving very
much as humans, while the second is made up of lively pictures of
horses, cows, falcons, chickens, and so on. The third is divided into
two parts, the first being a comedy with human actors, and the
other a caricature resembling the first scroll. The fourth and final
scroll is composed primarily of pictures of human beings playing
yabusame (a sport in which the contestants shoot arrows at a target
while riding horses), polo, *go,* backgammon, and other games. From
the stylistic point of view, the first two scrolls are noteworthy for
their vigorous, articulate lines, which mark them as the work of
a late Heian artist. By comparison, the other two scrolls seem relatively studied and restrained, and one is inclined to regard them
as a Kamakura addition. The entire painting has frequently been
ascribed to the Archbishop Kakuyû (1053–1140), but while this
eminent cleric may perhaps have drafted the first two scrolls, he
could hardly have had any connection with the later ones.

66

FROLIC OF THE ANIMALS *(detail)*
From the first of four paper scrolls in black and white. (See explanation for the previous plate.)

PLATE 12 SCROLL PAINTING

KAMAKURA PERIOD [1185—1338]

HANDBOOK ON ILLNESSES *(detail)*
One paper scroll in color. Height: 26.1 cm. Owner: The Sekido
Collection, Aichi Prefecture.

This scroll consists of pictures that show people suffering from
miscellaneous illnesses. In addition to the version in the Sekido
Collection, which comprises fifteen individual scenes and has been
preserved in scroll form, there are fragmentary sections of other
versions in the Tokyo National Museum and other repositories. The
part reproduced in this plate shows a man whose discomfort is that
all of his teeth are loose. In the other sections of the scroll, there
appear a man who is slightly blind, another who is tormented by body
lice, a woman whose breath is foul, and such like. The afflicted is in
each case accompanied by two or three persons who view with
an appropriate reaction the comedy or tragedy of his malady. The
sketches are wholly without compassion. The painter suggested no
remedy for the ailments, nor, indeed, did he seem to regard them
with any more amiable sentiment than one of cynical amusement.
His purpose was simply to give a vivid description. This was the age
of the "Handbook on Hells," the "Handbook on Hungry Ghosts," and
other grotesque paintings representing the underworlds of Buddhist
lore. The world of mankind too was held by Buddhists to be one of
the stages of suffering and futility, and the diseases that beset men
were but their just punishment for evil actions in previous incarnations. The "Handbook on Illnesses" is firmly rooted in this mode
of thinking.

70

PLATE 13 SCROLL PAINTING

KAMAKURA PERIOD [1185—1338]

THE STORY OF TOMO NO DAINAGON *(detail)*
From the first of three paper scrolls in color. 31.5×925.1 cm. Owner:
  The Sakai Collection, Tokyo.

This work, which depicts an anecdote in the *Tales from Uji (Uji Shûi Monogatari)*, is possibly the greatest of Japanese scroll paintings. The first of the three scrolls lacks the text of the story, but each of the other two is composed of a short passage from the text followed by a long illustrative painting. Actually, the pictorial sections are in such detail that the written portions are hardly needed to follow the plot.

The story is as follows: The Great Councillor *(dainagon)* Tomo Yoshio, in order to ensnare his political rival, the Minister of the Left, Minamoto Nobu, set fire to one of the imperial palace gates and deceitfully reported that Minamoto had committed the arson. The truth, however, was discovered, and in the end Tomo was banished for his crime. The first scroll, from which this plate is taken, depicts the burning of the gate. The artist's sketchy, impressionistic treatment of the tumultuous scene is forceful and penetrating.

"The History of Mt. Shigi" *(Plate 9)* has been cited above as a classic example of dynamic expression, but even greater movement is to be found here. At the same time, the coloring on the human figures shows signs of having originally been quite thick, and some of the interior scenes have a voluptuousness reminiscent of the *Tale of Genji* scrolls *(Plate 7)*. Consequently, the style of this painting may be thought of as a synthesis of the vivacious linear treatment seen in "The History of Mt. Shigi," and the quiet, colorful approach that characterizes the *tsukuri-e*. It is to be observed, however, that the accent in the present work is always on movement and speed. The artist is traditionally said to have been Fujiwara Mitsunaga, a leading painter of the twelfth century.

72

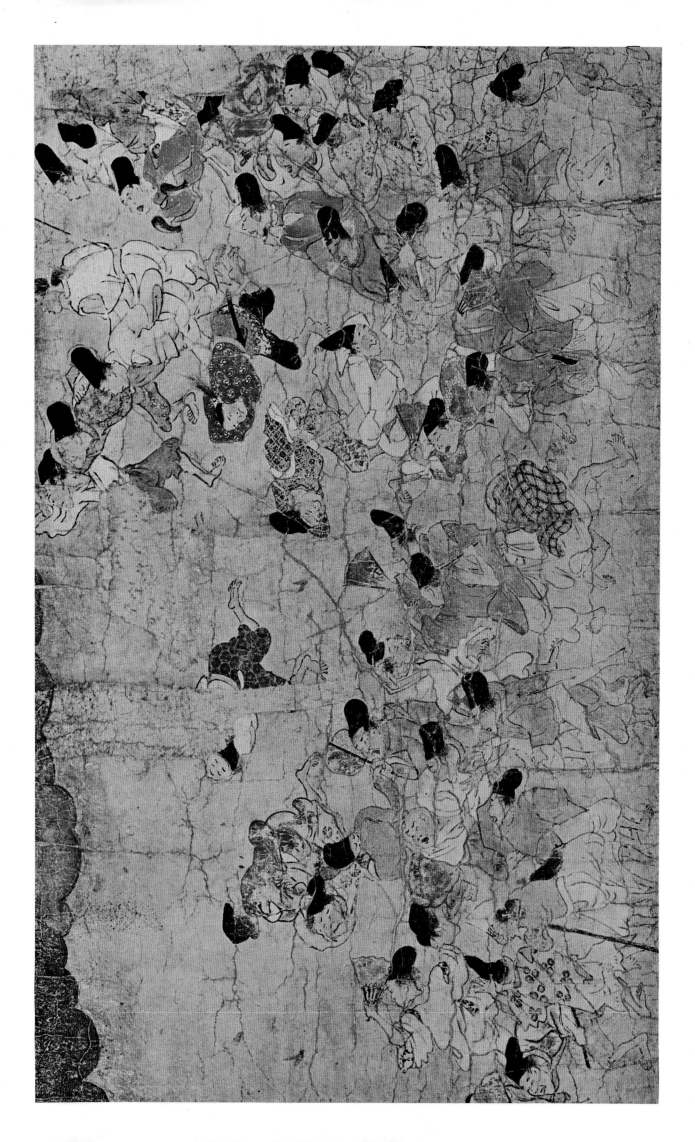

PLATE 14 SCROLL PAINTING

KAMAKURA PERIOD [1185—1338]

ILLUSTRATED *PILLOW BOOK* OF SEI SHÔNAGON *(detail)*
*One paper scroll in black and white. 25.5×998.4 cm. Owner: **The***
Asano Collection, Kanagawa Prefecture.

The scroll from which this plate is taken is a well-known work of
the late Kamakura period. It is composed of seven excerpts from
Sei Shônagon's celebrated *Pillow Book (Makura no Sôshi)*, with
accompanying illustrations in the *yamato-e* style. Except for the lips
of the human figures, which are painted in red, the pictures are black
monochromes. The hair and eyebrows of the people, as well as the
decorative patterns on the furnishings in the rooms, were drawn
with a rather dry brush to produce an effect of shading. Throughout
the work, the lines are so delicate as to suggest fine silk threads.

This work belongs in a sense to the tradition of the "Frolic of the
Animals" *(Plates 10 and 11)*. Here, however, the black-and-white lines
are unmodulated, and the underlying aesthetic concept is the same
as that which inspired the richly colored Genji scrolls *(Plate 7)*.

From an early time, the delicacy and intricacy with which this
painting was drafted led to the belief that the artist was a woman.
The calligraphy, on the other hand, is thought to have been done
by the Emperor Go-Kôgon (reigned 1351–1371 in the northern court,
which is not accepted as legitimate by some Japanese historians).

74

PLATE 15   SCROLL PAINTING

KAMAKURA PERIOD [1185—1338]

THE STORY OF THE LATTER THREE YEARS' CAMPAIGN *(detail)*
Three paper scrolls in color. 45.5×1968.3 cm. Owner: The Commission for the Protection of Cultural Properties, Tokyo.

From 1089 to 1091, Minamoto no Yoshiie, an ancestor of Yoritomo, carried on a sanguinary punitive war on behalf of the court against a powerful rebel in northern Japan. This expedition is usually termed the "Latter Three Years' Campaign" to distinguish it from a somewhat earlier war of similar nature, which is known as the "Former Nine Years' Campaign." Yoshiie, who finally succeeded in quelling the insurrection, is one of the most celebrated warriors in Japanese history and a model of the virtues that are thought becoming to that class. It is said that during the campaign in question he was about to lead his troops through the difficult approach to an enemy stronghold when he saw a flock of wild geese rise in confusion and correctly inferred an ambush in time to save his men. This story is depicted in the painting from which this plate is taken.

"The Story of the Latter Three Years' Campaign" now comprises only three scrolls, but it is clear that there were originally four, since the text as it now reads does not give the beginning of the narrative. Each of the scrolls is composed of a series of five written passages with accompanying illustrations. The action seems somewhat sluggish for a battle scene, but the work as a whole is still to be classed in the dynamic tradition of "The History of Mt. Shigi."

76

PLATE 16 PAINTING

KAMAKURA PERIOD [1185—1338]

PORTRAIT OF MINAMOTO NO YORITOMO *(detail)*
In color on silk. 139.4×111.9 cm. Owner: Jingo-ji, Kyoto.

Preserved in the Jingo-ji, a monastery in Kyoto, are four famous portraits that date from the beginning of the Kamakura period. The subjects were Taira no Shigemori, Fujiwara Mitsuyoshi, the priest Mongaku Shônin, and Minamoto no Yoritomo, the last of whom is shown here. A history of the Jingo-ji, dated 1328, states that the portraits were by the "Director of the Right Ward of the Capital," Fujiwara Takanobu (1142–1205), and there is little reason to suppose that this attribution is erroneous.

Yoritomo, clad in ceremonial cap and robe, is seated in a solemn pose. As shown here, his facial features are delineated in penetrating detail. The artist obviously intended to draw exactly what he saw— a living human being—and he succeeded. Here we see the stylistic perfection of the Japanese memorial portrait; that is to say, the class of likenesses which were intended to preserve the living form of the subject, as opposed to those which purported to beatify high priests or immortalize historical personages.

78

PLATE 17 PAINTING

KAMAKURA PERIOD [1185—1338]

Kôbô Daishi as a Boy *(detail)*
In color on silk. 77×39.4 cm. Owner: The Murayama Collection,
Hyôgo Prefecture.

This portrait is based on a tradition concerning the great Japanese
Buddhist patriarch Kûkai, better known as Kôbô Daishi. According
to the story, as a child the priest had a dream in which he saw himself
seated on an eight-petal lotus flower conversing with the Buddha.
Here this boyhood vision is simply and realistically portrayed. A lovely
child kneels on a lotus blossom, his palms held together in a holy
gesture, and his whole figure surrounded by a halo. His face has been
drawn in unusual detail, great care having been taken to give life to
his eyes, eyebrows, and lips. Similarly, the strands of his hair have
been painstakingly delineated, and we are even able to see a tip of
his ear. Tasteful use of gold and silver paint adds to the beauty of
the lifelike color tones.

It was a fashion in the late Heian and early Kamakura periods
to portray the Bodhisattvas Monju (Manjusri) and Fugen
(Samantabhadra) as children paying devotion to the Buddha, and
one is inclined to regard the present portrait as stemming from that
practice. In this case, however, the date can hardly have been earlier
than the middle years of the Kamakura period, for the techniques
employed are typical of that epoch. It should be noted that this
work, unlike many Kamakura likenesses, appears to have been
intended as an object of worship rather than merely as a portrait.

80

PLATE 18 SCROLL PAINTING

KAMAKURA PERIOD [1185—1338]

The Thirty-six Immortal Poets *(section showing Ko Ôgimi)*
In color on paper. Section: 35.8×59.7 cm. Owner: Yamato Bunka-kan, Osaka.

In the time of the Emperor Ichijô (reigned 987–1011), the poet Fujiwara Kintô (966–1041) compiled an anthology of poems by thirty-six men and women who excelled in vernacular poetry. Around the end of the Heian period and the beginning of the Kamakura period, these bards became so popular as subjects for painters that portraits of them came to constitute a special category, called "immortal-poet pictures" *(kasen-e)*. This sketch of the poetess Ko Ôgimi is from the earliest and best known work of this genre, a series of portraits in two scrolls said to have been painted by Fujiwara Nobuzane (1176–1265 ?). Both scrolls were for a long time the property of the Satake family, but in 1919 they were cut up into individual pictures, and at present they are divided among a number of collections. In contrast to other works of the same class, however, they are still known collectively as the "Satake version."

In the classic form of the "immortal-poet pictures," the name and court rank of the subject, together with a sample poem and a brief biography, appear to the right of the portrait. This is true of the present painting, although the writing is not shown here. In the case of a feminine subject, such as the one at hand, the coloring is usually rich, but in the case of men, it is frequently quite faint. In any event, the treatment is highly impressionistic. It furnishes an interesting contrast to the realism seen in the portrait of Minamoto no Yoritomo shown above *(Plate 16)*.

82

PLATE 19 PAINTING

MUROMACHI PERIOD [1338—1573]

HAN-SHAN
*By Ka-ô (fourteenth century). Kakemono, painted in ink on paper.
97.7×34 cm. Owner: Nagao Museum, Kanagawa Prefecture.*

The life and career of Ka-ô Ninga, one of the first Japanese painters
of ink monochromes, are almost totally obscure. One theory says he
was identical with Ka-ô Sônen, a priest of the Kannin-ji, who died
in 1345, but this cannot be accepted without reservation.

Japanese monochrome art was at first closely associated with Zen
Buddhism, and the earliest paintings dealt with Zen subjects, depicted
in the symbolic, simplified manner seen here. Han-shan was a Chinese
Zen priest of the T'ang dynasty, famous for his intuitive wisdom and
his poetry, as well as for his eccentric behavior. He is most often
represented in the company of his fellow priest Shih-tê. Their lives
appear to be quite legendary, but they are favorite subjects of Zen
painters. This is among the best of the many imaginative likenesses
of Han-shan.

PLATE 20 PAINTING

MUROMACHI PERIOD [1338—1573]

Man Catching a Catfish with a Gourd
By Josetsu (early fifteenth century). Kakemono, painted in ink on paper. 119.6×76.2 cm. Owner: Taizô-in, Kyoto.

Josetsu is the most famous of the early Japanese monochrome artists, but little is known about his life other than that he was a Zen priest of the Shôkoku-ji in Kyoto. The painting shown here is the only work definitely proven to be his. The inscription on it states that it was painted "in the new style" on the order of the shogun Ashikaga Yoshimochi and was to be kept always near the shogun's seat. The "new style" mentioned here is usually interpreted to mean that of the monochrome landscape, which was still unfamiliar at the time.

The painting is of the class known as *zenki,* or "Zen devices," which, as the name indicates, were intended primarily as aids to attaining Zen enlightenment. They included both portraits of famous priests and representations of stories or events that were considered inspirational. This work at hand is of the latter category, but it has many of the qualities of a pure landscape.

PLATE 21 PAINTING

MUROMACHI PERIOD [1338—1573]

WINTER LANDSCAPE
*By Sesshû (1420–1506). From a pair of kakemono called "Autumn
and Winter Landscapes," painted in ink on paper. 46.4×29.4 cm.
each. Owner: Tokyo National Museum.*

Sesshû was the greatest Japanese painter of ink monochromes in the
Sung style and at the same time the true founder of Japanese
landscape art. At an early age he became a priest at the Shôkoku-in,
where he likely studied under Shûbun. In 1468, he made a journey
to China, remaining there for a year, with the result that his Chinese-
style landscapes ring truer than those of most contemporary Japanese
artists, who knew continental scenery only at second hand. After
returning, he traveled about to various districts in Japan, but it
appears that after 1486 he settled down at the Unkoku-an, a temple
in Suô, where he died in 1506.

The present landscape is one of a pair originally preserved at the
Manju-in in Kyoto. It is among the most representative of Sesshû's
works.

88

PLATE 22 PAINTING

MUROMACHI PERIOD [1338—1573]

HABOKU LANDSCAPE
By Sesshû (1420–1506). Kakemono, painted in ink on paper. 149×33 cm. Owner: Tokyo National Museum.

The term *haboku* translated character by character means "broken ink," and this meaning does not sound too farfetched when one considers the near-abstraction shown here. While the word dates back to the T'ang dynasty in China, however, its actual etymology and significance are open to question, and we have chosen simply to use the Japanese transliteration here.

This diminutive landscape, certainly one of the true masterworks of Oriental art, was painted by Sesshû for his disciple Sôen in 1496 and therefore represents the artist's most mature years.

90

PLATE 23 PAINTING

MUROMACHI PERIOD [1338—1573]

CHOU MAO-SHU VIEWING THE LOTUS FLOWERS
By Kanô Masanobu (1434–1530). Kakemono, painted in color on paper. 279×109 cm. Owner: Mr. Tomijirô Nakamura, Tokyo.

Chou Mao-shu was a Chinese Confucian scholar of the Sung period (960–1279). It is said that he was a man of quiet personality, who resigned from governmental office, took up a secluded life at the foot of a mountain called Lu-shan, and spent his days admiring the lotus flowers in a nearby lake. He has been a favorite subject of Japanese painters. The present treatment is one of the two known works of Kanô Masanobu, from whom the Kanô School descended.

History records that Masanobu was named Official Governmental Artist for the Ashikaga shogunate in 1467, and that he painted numerous landscapes and portraits. He was the first professional painter in Japan to work in the style of Sung China, which had until his time been more or less monopolized by Zen priests.

PLATE 24 PAINTING

MUROMACHI PERIOD [1338—1573]

Storm at Sea
By Sesson (1504–1589 ?). Kakemono, painted in ink with slight
coloring on paper. 22.2×31.4 cm. Owner: Mr. Fumihide Nomura,
Kyoto.

This diminutive painting of a rough sea is not only Sesson's greatest
masterpiece, but one of the most striking ink monochromes ever
produced in Japan.

Sesson was born in 1504 in Hitachi Province (modern Ibaragi
Prefecture). He called himself a "pupil of Sesshû," but, of course,
he could not have studied directly under Sesshû, since he was only
two when the latter died. His style, however, closely resembles that
of his illustrious predecessor.

Nothing is known of his career save that he was a Zen priest, and
that he lived most, if not all, of his life in his native area. He died
around 1589, but the exact year is uncertain. His paintings are often
criticized as "eccentric," but the present work is quite orthodox in
both content and treatment.

94

PLATE 25 PAINTING

LATE MUROMACHI PERIOD [1338—1573]

MAPLE-VIEWERS AT MT. TAKAO
By Kanô Hideyori (middle of the sixteenth century). From a six-panel folding screen, painted in color on paper. 149×364 cm. Owner: Tokyo National Museum.

The landscape from which this detail is taken is historically important for two reasons. In the first place, it combined both Chinese and Japanese elements in a manner that anticipated the style of Kanô Eitoku and other Momoyama artists, and in the second, it contains sections, such as the one shown, which were among the earliest fore-runners of the genre art of the Edo period.

In the background of this autumnal scene there are snow-capped mountain peaks suggesting winter, and it is consequently thought that this screen was one of a pair based on the four seasons, a favorite subject of *yamato-e* painters from Heian times on. Such works frequently showed the seasonal festivities and celebrations of the common people, but no earlier example than that seen here reveals so much emphasis on individuals. In this respect the painting may be taken as a reflection of the growing economic power and rising social status of plebeians.

96

PLATE 26 PAINTING

MOMOYAMA PERIOD [1573—1615]

CELEBRATION UNDER THE CHERRY BLOSSOMS *(detail)*
By Kanô Naganobu (1577–1654). From a pair of six-panel folding
screens, painted in color on paper. 194.4×356.1 cm. each. Owner:
Mr. Kunizô Hara, Kanagawa Prefecture.

The subject of the painting in which this detail appears is a picnic
under the cherry blossoms—an annual pastime fashionable among
the Japanese during the Momoyama period and since. In this case,
the women shown are probably not commoners, as was later frequently the case, but members of the samurai class.

The artist, Kanô Naganobu, was a grandson of Motonobu and
a son of Naonobu. His existing works are very few, and the present
pair of screens are the only ones that bear his seal. This makes them
particularly important, since most early genre paintings are unsigned
and unidentifiable by style.

The dancing ladies seem lovely and lively, but while the occasion
is obviously a happy one, the painting has the dignity that one would
expect from a member of the prestigious Kanô School.

PLATE 27 PAINTING

MOMOYAMA PERIOD [1573—1615]

PLUM TREE
By Kanô Eitoku (1543–1590). Four door panels, painted in ink on paper. Height: 175.2 cm. each. Owner: Jukô-in, Kyoto.

Kanô Eitoku was the most celebrated of the painters who worked in the grandiose Momoyama style. A protégé of the military dictators Oda Nobunaga and Toyotomi Hideyoshi, he was commissioned to decorate the walls and door panels in most of the great castles and palaces of his time. Unfortunately, most of the paintings he produced, together with the colossal buildings that they adorned, have been lost.

Sixteen paintings on door panels in the Jukô-in are among the very few considered to be his genuine works. Thought to have been painted in about 1566 when the Jukô-in was built, they include two groups, one depicting the "four accomplishments" *(see the explanation to Plate 32)* and the other comprising a number of landscapes and flower-and-bird pictures. The former set is executed more or less in the style of Motonobu, but in the latter Eitoku reveals a strong personal inclination toward boldness and gorgeousness. Especially remarkable is the single plum tree shown here, which spreads over four large panels (the fourth panel, not shown here, extends to the left). This gigantic composition is a pioneer work among the murals of the Momoyama period. Curves and angles such as those composing the trunk and branches of the tree were to be found in Motonobu's paintings, but here they are more highly emphasized. They form a distinguishing characteristic of Eitoku's art. Though in black and white, the present painting is much more decorative than even the colored paintings of the preceding Muromachi period.

100

PLATE 28 PAINTING

MOMOYAMA PERIOD [1573—1615]

PINE TREES
By Hasegawa Tôhaku (1539–1610). Pair of six-panel folding screens, painted in ink on paper. 156×346 cm. Owner: Tokyo National Museum.

Hasegawa Tôhaku was one of the greatest Momoyama period rivals of the Kanô School. Born in Noto Province (Ishikawa Prefecture), he studied painting at the Kôryû-ji in Kyoto and later came to refer to himself as "Sesshû the Fifth." He was a very versatile painter, able to use both Chinese and Japanese styles either in color or in black and white.

The present screen, which shows pine trees swaying in a drizzling rain, is executed entirely in varying tones of black. The daring abbreviation and bold spacing are unique among the paintings of Tôhaku's time. They reflect his ambition to parallel Mu Ch'i, a Chinese priest-painter of the Sung dynasty, whom he held in particularly high esteem. Beside the spiritual aloofness of Mu Ch'i, however, the art of Tôhaku seems soft and lyrical.

102

PLATE 29   PAINTING

EARLY EDO PERIOD [1615—1867]

SHRIKE ON A DEAD BRANCH
By Miyamoto Musashi (1584–1645). Kakemono, painted in ink on
paper. 125.6×54.3 cm. Owner: Nagao Museum, Kanagawa Pre-
fecture.

Miyamoto Musashi, whose art name is Niten, is more famous as
a valiant swordsman than as a painter, but he left a collection of
more than ten ink monochromes that are among the most spirited
Japanese works in that idiom. He was especially adept in the use of
the abbreviated "reduced-stroke" *(gempitsu)* technique developed by
the Sung artist Liang K'ai. As the name implies, this calls for sketchy,
cryptic outlines, usually drawn with great speed and force. A better
example than the painting shown here could hardly be found. One's
attention is immediately captured by the tense resilient line forming
the center of the composition, but the remainder of the work shows
the same sure command of the brush. Musashi's favorite subjects
were strong, shrewd birds like the shrike, the cormorant, and the
fighting cock. Perhaps they appealed to his warrior tastes.

PLATE 30 PAINTING

EDO PERIOD [1615—1867]

MIOTSUKUSHI

By Tawaraya Sôtatsu (early seventeenth century). From a pair of six-panel folding screens based on the Tale of Genji, *painted in color in paper, 157×263 cm. each. Owner: Seika-dô Foundation, Tokyo.*

This screen and its companion piece are the greatest among the many works attributed to Sôtatsu. They are based on the chapters in the *Tale of Genji* entitled "Sekiya" and "Miotsukushi." The scene shown here is one in which the hero Genji happens to meet with a former lover, Akashi Himegimi, near the Shinto shrine of Sumiyoshi.

Sôtatsu's works are characterized by flat spreads of color, often without contour lines, and bold linear patterns. Much has been written of his use of a new technique called *tarashikomi,* whereby drops of color or water were added to the original coloring before the latter had dried, but this was simply a new application of an old idea, since essentially the same method was employed in the *haboku* ink paintings *(see Plate 22).* The general composition and the color scheme of works such as the one at hand, however, mark the beginning of a new epoch in the history of Japanese painting. Though the subject is from an ancient romance, the painting is not simply a graphic aid to understanding the story, but an independent work of art. Herewith the *yamato-e* is freed from the bonds imposed by literature.

Despite Sôtatsu's great fame, few facts concerning his life are known. He is said to have been born to the family of either a textile dealer or a fan dealer in Kyoto and to have been active during the Keichô and Genna eras (1596–1623). He lived at Takagamine, a northern suburb of Kyoto, in a community of artists and art lovers centered around Hon'ami Kôetsu, a versatile and well-known aesthete, to whom he probably owed much of his style.

106

PLATE 31 PAINTING

EARLY SEVENTEENTH CENTURY

WESTERNERS PLAYING MUSIC
*Artist unknown. From a pair of six-panel folding screens, painted
in color on paper. 93×302 cm. each. Owner: Mr. Mokichi Okada,
Shizuoka Prefecture.*

Contact with Portuguese culture in the second half of the sixteenth
century led to the imitation of Western painting. At first works in
the exotic style were concerned exclusively with Christian propaganda,
but as Western ways became somewhat more familiar, painters began
to deal with non-religious subjects as well, modeling their works to
a great extent on imported pictures. Western-style shading and
perspective had previously been unknown in Japan, and the Japanese
artists failed at times in their attempts to utilize them. It is interesting
to note that they tried by using nut oil and pigment obtained from
clay to produce the effect of Western oil painting. The name of the
artist who made this pair of screens is unknown, but most likely he
was a young painter who had taken a regular course in Western
painting in a Christian school. The painting probably dates from the
second decade of the seventeenth century.

108

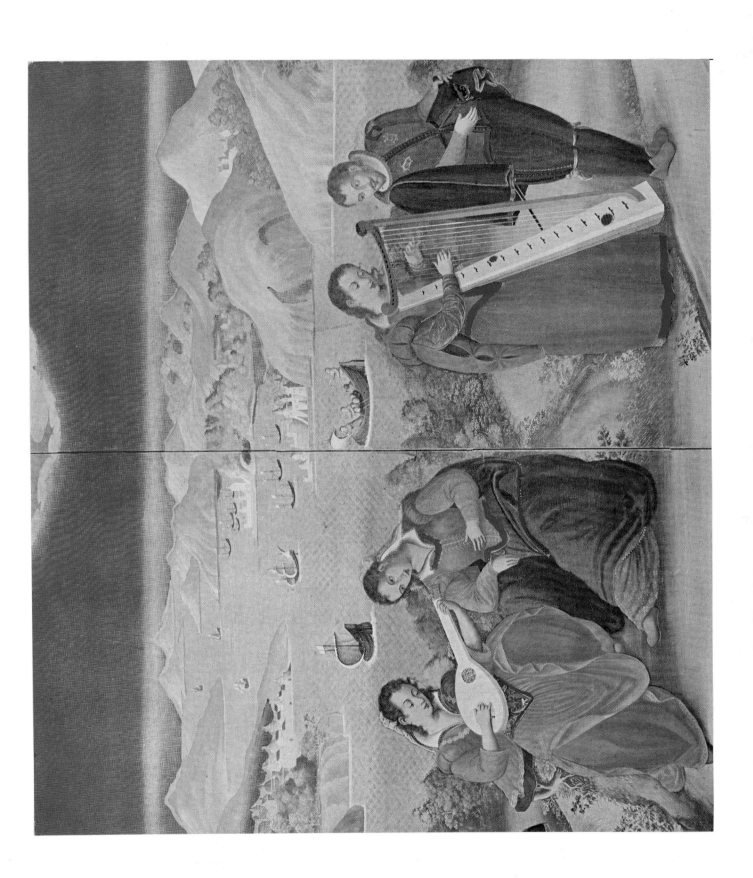

PLATE 32   PAINTING

EDO   PERIOD   [1615—1867]

THE FOUR ACCOMPLISHMENTS
By Kanô Tan'yû (1602–1674). Formerly mounted on a wall of the Jôraku-den in Nagoya Castle, Aichi Prefecture.

The "four accomplishments" are playing the lute, playing *go*, painting, and writing, or, in other words, music, elegant pastimes, art, and learning. These were the fields of cultural attainment in which the gentlemen of the Tokugawa period sought to excel.

The present painting was in the Jôraku-den, a palace built in 1634 for the use of Tokugawa Iemitsu. The walls and doors of this building were all decorated by Kanô Tan'yû, or more probably by a group of painters headed by him. Unfortunately the paintings were destroyed along with the building itself in a World War II air raid.

Tan'yû, the son of Kanô Takanobu (1571–1618), left the family home at Kyoto and went to Edo in about 1617 at the invitation of the Tokugawa government. In 1621 he was named chief artist to the shogun and given an official residence near the Kajibashi gateway to the Edo Castle. His descendants are therefore called the Kajibashi Kanô, as distinct from the Kyô Kanô, who trace their ancestry to Kanô Sanraku. Tan'yû's was a steady, diligent personality, and the found his most suitable artistic medium in such dignified subjects as that shown here.

110

PLATE 33 PAINTING

EDO PERIOD [1615—1867]

IRISES

By Ogata Kôrin (1658–1716). From a pair of six-panel folding screens, painted in color on paper. 150.6×358.2 cm. Owner: Nezu Museum, Tokyo.

Ogata Kôrin was the greatest Edo period exponent of Sôtatsu's decorative style, and the painting shown here is one of his most outstanding works. Its subject is derived from a poem in the *Tales of Ise (Ise Monogatari)* about the irises blooming near the celebrated Eightfold Bridge in Mikawa Province. The treatment is exceedingly simple—the bridge is omitted, and the marsh in which the plants are growing is represented by a plain gold background, while the flowers and leaves are in ordinary shades of blue and green. Kôrin often painted as here without contour lines, this feature being one of the distinguishing marks of the Sôtatsu style.

Like many others of the same tradition, Kôrin was a versatile craftsman as well as a painter. On one of his most successful pieces of lacquer ware *(Plate 81)*, he used essentially the same design as that seen here.

112

PLATE 34 PAINTING

EDO PERIOD [1615—1867]

SUMMER AND AUTUMN PLANTS
*By Sakai Hôitsu (1761–1828). From a pair of two-panel folding
screens, painted in color on paper covered with silver leaf.
164×182 cm. each. Owner: Mr. Muneyoshi Tokugawa, Tokyo.*

Sakai Hôitsu was the second son of the feudal lord who ruled over
the Himeji fief, but he gave up the life of a privileged samurai for
that of an artist. He studied several different styles of painting before
finally settling on that of Kôrin, but once he had made his choice
he proved himself to be the most faithful of Kôrin's followers. It is
interesting to note that he was separated from his exemplar by
a century, just as the latter had been from Sôtatsu. The relation
between the three is unique among Edo schools of art, in which as
a rule the lineage was maintained by a sort of apostolic succession.

The work illustrated here is one of two paintings done on the
reverse sides of a pair of screens by Kôrin. It shows Hôitsu's style at
its best.

114

PLATE 35   PAINTING

EDO PERIOD [1615—1867]

CONVENIENCE OF FARMING
*By Ike no Taiga (1723–1776).   Painted in ink with slight coloring
on paper.   17.7×17.7 cm.   Owner: Mr. Yasunari Kawabata, Kanagawa Prefecture.*

The Chinese poet Li Li-wêng lived in a small hermitage at the foot
of a mountain. Once he was visited by a friend who, by way of
expressing sympathy, spoke of the inconvenience of life in the country.
Far from being grateful, Li was moved to answer with a set of
extemporaneous poems on what he called the "ten conveniences and
ten joys" of rural living. The ten "conveniences" were cultivating the
land, drawing water, washing, supplying water for the garden, angling,
reciting poems out loud, performing the farm tasks, obtaining fuel
wood, being safe and quiet at night, and seeing fine sights. The ten
"joys" were the views of the scenery in the four seasons, at dawn and
in the evening, and in fine, windy, cloudy, and rainy weather. In
1771 Ike no Taiga and Yosa Buson (1716–1783) painted a series of
pictures illustrating these. The "Ten Conveniences," by Taiga are
marked by bold composition and unconventional brushwork, while
the "Ten Joys," by Buson have a pronounced lyric quality. The
"Convenience of Performing the Farm Tasks," reproduced here, is
the best of Taiga's group. It seems very modern, both in brushwork
and in coloring.

116

課農便

山甸四面總玲瓏綠野青疇一望中

農力盡何曾妨却讀書工

憑几課農

FIG 1

PLATE 36 PAINTING

EDO PERIOD [1615—1867]

A SUNNY MORNING AT UJI
By Aoki Mokubei (1767–1833). Kakemono, painted in color on
paper. 50×60.7 cm. Owner: Commission for the Protection of
Cultural Properties, Tokyo.

The setting is the River Uji, south of Kyoto, at sunrise. To the left
is the famous bridge of Uji, to the right the Phoenix Hall of the
Byôdô-in *(Plate 90)*, and in the background a distant mountain
range. It seems that Mokubei was very fond of this scene, for he
painted several landscapes based on it. This one, which is the best
among them, is a fine example of the softness with which painters
of the Nanga School treated nature. It has an inscription by the
artist dated 1824, the year in which he was fifty-seven.

Mokubei was known particularly as a potter, but he was also
a master of painting, calligraphy, and poetry. He was intimately
friendly with such well-known men of art and letters as Rai Sanyô
and Tanomura Chikuden.

118

PLATE 37 PAINTING

EDO PERIOD [1615—1867]

WOMAN
*By Hishikawa Moronobu (1618–1694). Painted in color on silk.
36.0×31.2 cm. Owner: Tokyo National Museum.*

This is one of the comparatively rare paintings of the artist who is
credited with having originated the *ukiyo-e* print. It is very likely
the portrait of one of the charmers in the gay quarters of Yoshiwara
so often depicted by later *ukiyo-e* artists. The strong lines and simple
coloring are typical of early *ukiyo-e,* while the long face and torso of
the woman represent contemporary ideals of feminine beauty.

120

PLATE 38 WOODBLOCK PRINT

EDO PERIOD [1615—1867]

WOMAN ON A VERANDA
By Suzuki Harunobu (1725–1770). 26.4×19.8 cm. Owner: Mr. Takaharu Mitsui.

Harunobu was the first artist to produce the multicolored prints known as *nishiki-e,* or "brocade pictures." Until his time red and green had been the only colors, but a technique he invented allowed for the use of ten or more.

Not only his color schemes, but his subjects as well, were more complicated than those of his predecessors. He excelled particularly at drawing young men and women of incredibly graceful figure, more often than not in amorous scenes. Their elongated, delicately curved bodies are a distinctive mark of his work.

122

PLATE 39 WOODBLOCK PRINT

EDO PERIOD [1615—1867]

THE FICKLE TYPE
By Kitagawa Utamaro (1753–1806). From "Ten Physiognomical Studies of Women." Printed on paper. 37.9×26.4 cm. Owner: Tokyo National Museum.

Of all the *ukiyo-e* artists Utamaro was the most successful in portraying beautiful women, for, unlike his predecessors, he focused his attention on their physical features instead of their clothing or the settings in which they appeared.

Only four or five of the set known as "Ten Physiognomical Studies of Women" exist, but there is a like number of similar prints that the artist published under the title "Women of Ten Physiognomical Types" and it is thought that the two sets were intended as only one. Probably the title was changed after half the prints had been published. The example shown here appeared in 1791.

Utamaro succeeded Torii Kiyonaga as the dominant figure in the *ukiyo-e* field, but success seems to have gone to his head. His works gradually declined in artistic value, and he spent the latter years of his life in a continual state of ill temper, ranting at publishers and belittling the works of other artists. Perhaps he was suffering from frustration. An old and ugly man, he could hardly have been loved by women such as those he envisioned.

124

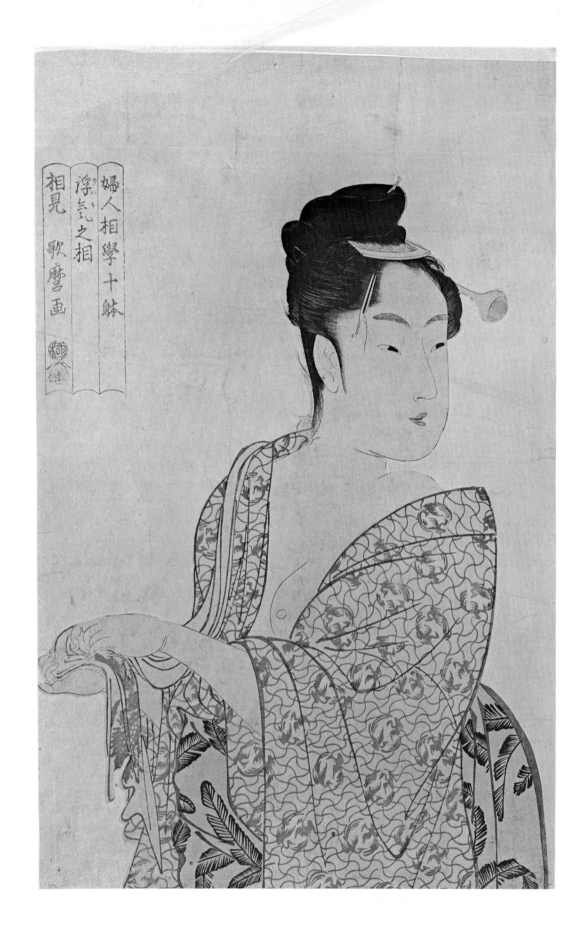

PLATE 40 WOODBLOCK PRINT

EDO PERIOD [1615—1867]

THE ACTOR BANDÔ MITSUGORÔ
*By Tôshûsai Sharaku (active 1794–95). 39×26 cm. Owner: Tokyo
National Museum.*

Sharaku is a mystery. Nothing is known about him except that his
real name was Saitô Jûrobei, that he might have been a Noh actor
employed by Lord Hachisuka of Awa Province, and that he lived
at Hatchô-bori in Edo. The period of his artistic activity was
exceedingly short. In May, 1794, he published his first pictures, in
which he portrayed actors of the three main Kabuki theaters in Edo.
Later he made prints for Kabuki performances in August and
November of the same year and February of the following. During
this interval of ten months he produced one hundred and forty
pictures in all.

His specialities were close-ups and full-length portraits of Kabuki
actors, which he painted in an impressionistic style immediately
distinguishable from that of other *ukiyo-e* artists. The example given
here shows the actor Bandô Mitsugorô as he appeared in the role of
Ishii Genzô in May, 1794.

126

坂東三津五郎

甲寅九月

PLATE 41 WOODBLOCK PRINT

EDO PERIOD [1615—1867]

THE RED FUJI
By Katsushika Hokusai (1760–1849). 39×26 cm. From the series
entitled "Thirty-six Views of Mt. Fuji." Owner: Tokyo National
Museum.

Hokusai is known as the inventor of the Japanese landscape print,
which has been such a great source of inspiration to modern Western
artists. His most famous work is a series known as "Thirty-six Views
of Mt. Fuji," from which the picture shown here is taken. The whole
set, which was published between 1825 and 1832, is actually composed
of forty-six prints, thirty-six showing the mountain from the east
and ten from the west. Not a human being is to be seen in this print
or its companion piece, "Fuji in a Storm," which has almost the same
composition, but in the remainder of the prints people and animals
are fairly prominent. It is clear that Hokusai employed the mountain
to give perspective and stability to his views of changing, unpredictable
humanity. In this picture, however, the peak soars up into an infinite
sky—a silent giant, remote and secure from human interference. This
is perhaps the boldest of all the many Japanese representations of
the sacred mountain.

PLATE 42 PAINTING

EDO PERIOD [1615—1867]

BEAUTY *(detail)*
By Katsushika Hokusai (1760–1849). Kakemono, painted in color on silk. 99×30.1 cm. Owner: Mr. Moshichi Yoshihara.

One would never guess that this doll-like woman is a work of the landscape artist Hokusai. It is not, however, as foreign to his style as it might seem at first glance. In his landscapes, Hokusai used exaggerated forms, but was always in pursuit of reality. Similarly, in this work, he has endowed the woman with exaggerated delicacy, but has taken great care to copy the patterns on the clothing with perfect accuracy and even to try to convey the crinkly feel of the crepe neckband.

130

PLATE 43   WOODBLOCK PRINT

EDO PERIOD [1615—1867]

KAMBARA

By Andô Hiroshige (1797–1858). From the series "The Fifty-three Stages of the Tôkaidô." 39×26 cm. Owner: Tokyo National Museum.

While Hokusai was the creator of the Japanese landscape print, it was Hiroshige who explored the limits of its potentialities. The two artists have much in common, but whereas Hokusai was rational and objective, Hiroshige was poetic and idealistic.

The Tôkaidô was a highway running from Edo to the ancient capital Kyoto. It was divided into fifty-three stages, with a station at the end of each. In 1831, when the shogun sent a present of horses to the emperor, Hiroshige followed the envoy along the way, making sketches as he traveled. In the following year he published a series of fifty-five landscape prints showing a scene from each of the stages and the two terminals. This was his debut as an artist, but the work was so successful that he published more than ten similar sets on the same subject. The first, however, was never surpassed. It is from this that the print shown here is taken.

Having become famous by painting the Tôkaidô landscapes, Hiroshige ever afterward cherished the highway in his memory. Just before he died he composed the following farewell poem:

"I leave my brush in the East

And set forth on my journey.

I shall see the famous scenery of the Western Land."

The "Western Land" in the last line is a double reference to the western paradise of Amida and to Kyoto, which is west of Edo.

PLATE 44 SCULPTURE

PREHISTORIC PERIOD [—552]

HANIWA HEAD OF A GIRL
Height: 16.5 cm. Owner: Mr. Gakunan Matsubara, Tokyo.

This *haniwa* fragment was acquired by the owner's father in his native district, which was in ancient times the province of Yamato. The exact site of excavation is not known, but the piece certainly came from an ancient burial mound. To date, specimens of *haniwa* figures discovered in Yamato are much less numerous than those from the Kantô District in eastern Japan. They were made by essentially the same technique as the latter, but as a rule they show much more refined modeling.

134

PLATE 45   SCULPTURE

ASUKA PERIOD [552—645]

Shaka Nyorai (Sakyamuni)
From a Sakyamuni Triad by Tori, dated 623. Bronze. Height: Sakyamuni, seated, 86.5 cm. Attendants, standing, 90.0 cm. each. Placed in the main hall of the Hôryû-ji, Nara.

The inscription on the back of the halo states that this triad was made in the thirty-first year of the reign of the Empress Suiko (623) by the sculptor Kuratsukuribe no Tori, on the order of the consort and the son of Prince Shôtoku, as well as of various courtiers, to help secure the rebirth in Paradise of the prince, who had passed away in the preceding year.

The triad is mounted on a pedestal of wood, decorated with paintings in color. Sakyamuni, his two attendants (not visible here), their haloes, and the large halo for the entire triad, were each cast separately in one piece. They are all gilded, but the gilt is for the larger part concealed under coats of dirt.

Sakyamuni has the same iconographic form as Buddhas found in the Chinese rock-cave temples at Yün-kang, Lung-mên, and T'ien-lung-shan, which date from the period of the Northern and Southern Dynasties (420–589). He wears an undergarment hanging from the left shoulder down to the right side, a skirt with a belt fastened at the stomach, and an outer garment resembling a priest's robe. The Buddha and the large halo were probably cast by the wax-model technique, and surface details finished with a burin. This technique was often used in both the Asuka and Nara periods.

136

PLATE 46 SCULPTURE

ASUKA PERIOD [552—645]

KANNON BOSATSU (AVALOKITESVARA)
Wood. Height: 197 cm. Placed in the Yume-dono of the Hôryû-ji, Nara.

This statue is identical with the one described in the "Inventory of the Eastern Precinct of the Hôryû-ji," under the entry for the tenth month, 751, as "one wooden image of Kanzeon Bosatsu, of the same height as Prince Shôtoku and covered with gold leaf." It was enshrined in the Yume-dono in 739.

The entire figure was carved in one piece out of a single block of camphorwood, except for the lower ends of the long scarf. The surface is covered with gold leaf on calcium carbonate priming. The Bodhisattva holds a "sacred gem" and wears a crown of gilt bronze with beaded and perforated woodbine designs. The austere frontal treatment is very similar to that displayed in the Sakyamuni Triad in the main hall of the Hôryû-ji *(Plate 45)*. Both statues are derived from the style that prevailed in China during the Northern Wei dynasty (386–534), and both are typical of Asuka sculpture in all respects. Like the Sakyamuni, this may very well have been made by the famous sculptor Tori.

Since this is a "secret Buddha" *(hibutsu)*, shown only once a year, it is exceptionally well preserved.

138

PLATE 47 SCULPTURE

ASUKA PERIOD [552—645]

KUDARA KANNON (AVALOKITESVARA)
Wood. Height: 209.2 cm. Owner: Hôryû-ji, Nara.

Whereas the Kannon in the Yume-dono represents the style of Tori,
this statue is typical of the other style employed during the Asuka
period. The two are not categorically different, but a comparison of
the images reveals a number of important distinctions. The most
striking is that the work shown here is more three-dimensional and,
unlike the other, may be viewed to advantage from the side as well
as from the front. Other differences in detail add up to make this
the more plastic and graceful of the two works. However magnificent
the Yume-dono statue may be, it lacks a certain ethereal quality
found here.

The presence of Korean stylistic elements in this image have led
many to suppose that it was either imported from Korea or made
by a Korean artist, and indeed the popular name for it, "Kudara
Kannon," seems to support the supposition, Kudara being the
Japanese term for Pekché. Japanese authorities, however, are almost
unanimous in considering it an example of native art.

140

PLATE 48 SCULPTURE

ASUKA PERIOD [552—645]

Miroku Bosatsu (Maitreya)
Wood. Height: 133 cm. Owner: Chûgû-ji, Nara.

The statue, halo, and pedestal are all carved of camphorwood. The head is composed of two blocks, jointed vertically behind the ears, while the torso, the shins and the clothing hanging therefrom, the arms, and the left foot are all made separately. The statue now has a glossy black color, but it may originally have been colored or covered with gold leaf.

The pose, in which the right foot rests on the left knee and the right hand touches the cheek, is peculiar to ancient statues. Thanks to the beautifully rounded contours of the body and the free, flowing lines of the clothing, the effect is quite different from that of the austere Sakyamuni Triad in the Hôryû-ji *(Plate 45)*. The work is somewhat like the Kudara Kannon *(Plate 47)*, but is artistically more advanced.

The halo is in the so-called "sacred-jewel" shape. It has a lotus flower design in the center, and this is surrounded by flames, amid which are seven diminutive Buddhas.

This work is sometimes said to be Nyoirin Kannon (Cintamani), but most authorities identify it as Miroku.

142

PLATE 49 SCULPTURE

NARA PERIOD [645—794]

KANNON BOSATSU (AVALOKITESVARA)
*Bronze. Height: 190 cm. Placed in the Tôin-dô of the Yakushi-ji,
Nara.*

This statue and its pedestal were made separately by a very skillful
technique of bronze casting. The image itself was thickly gilded, but
the surface is now brownish-black with age. The amply modeled
figure, powerful yet graceful, reflects the fresh vigor of early T'ang
art, while the erect pose, full chest, and constricted waist, as well as
the clothing, are derived indirectly from Indian sculpture of the
Gupta period.

History offers no data regarding the exact age of this statue, but
it appears to be from about the same era as the Buddha head shown
in the next plate, that is, roughly, the late seventh century.

PLATE 50 SCULPTURE

NARA PERIOD [645—794]

BUDDHA HEAD
Bronze. Height: 106.8 cm. Owner: Kôfuku-ji, Nara.

This head was discovered in 1937 under the dais of the main statue in the principal building of the Kôfuku-ji. The statue to which it belonged is believed to have been made between 678 and 685 as the main icon for the lecture hall of the Yamada-dera and moved to the Kôfuku-ji in 1187, where it was destroyed in a fire caused by lightning in 1411. The head itself shows signs of having received a very heavy blow. The top back part is missing, and the forehead and left side are badly disfigured. What remains, however, is still quite beautiful. The cheeks are relatively full, the eyes elongated, the nose straight and strong, and the lips thick and proud. The style is derived from that of the early T'ang.

PLATE 51 SCULPTURE

NARA PERIOD [645—794]

AMIDA (AMITABHA) AND TWO ATTENDANTS
In Lady Tachibana's Shrine. Bronze. Height: Amida, 33.5 cm.
Attendants, 25.8 cm. Owner: Hôryû-ji, Nara.

This shrine is thought to date from the late seventh century and to
have belonged to Lady Tachibana, mother of the Empress Kômyô.
It consists of a miniature building covered by a roof similar to
canopies of the Asuka style and resting on a pedestal like that of the
Sakyamuni triad *(Plate 45)* in the main hall of the Hôryû-ji. The
floor under the triad is covered with sheet bronze on which there are
designs of rippling water and lotus leaves. Behind the images there is
a screen, also of bronze, with relief designs of Bodhisattvas seated on
lotus flowers, and, on the upper portion, of small Buddhas. Back of
the head of Amida there is a halo of bronze openwork.

The two attendants were cast in a piece with the inner parts of
their lotus flowers, as were the lotus stalks and outer rows of petals.
The lotus flower on which Amida is seated was made separately from
the figure itself.

The importance of these statues lies in the fact that they represent
a transition from the Asuka style to that of the Nara period. This
matter is discussed in the accompanying historical outline.

148

PLATE 52 SCULPTURE

NARA PERIOD [645—794]

FUKÛ KENSAKU KANNON (AMOGHAPASA)
Dry-lacquer. Height: 363.6 cm. In the Hokke-dô of the Tôdaiji,
Nara.

This statue is the principal icon of the Hokke-dô, the oldest extant
hall in the Tôdaiji, and it was probably made at the time of that
building's construction in the Tempyô epoch (729–749). Molded by
the dry-lacquer technique, it is one of the best remaining works in
the massive style of T'ang period art. The deity has three eyes and
six arms (only two can be seen in this plate), after the Indian
fashion, but they have a well-balanced, almost natural, appearance.
Except for a portion of the scarf on the right side, which has been
restored, the statue is very well preserved.

This silver crown is one of the finest pieces of metalwork from this
period. Its elaborate perforated design is supplemented by jewels
and beads. The over-all form of the headpiece is the same as it
originally was, but it has undergone repairs in places as well as a few
losses by theft. The nimbus, composed basically of concentric egg-
shaped curves against straight radial bars, is decorated here and there
with arabesques. The effect of the backpiece as a whole is quite
impressive, but the halo seems now to be a little lower than it ought
to be. The pedestal, which is of the "six-fold lotus" type, is heavy
enough to give the huge image a stable appearance. There are holes
on the front of the pedestal in which objects representing attributes
of the deity may once have been placed.

PLATE 53   SCULPTURE

NARA PERIOD [645—794]

Gakkô Butsu (Candraprabhasa)
*Clay.   Height: 204.8 cm.   Placed in the Hokke-dô of the Tôdaiji,
Nara.*

Gakkô and Nikkô, the Buddhas of the moon and the sun are now
enshrined on the altar in the Hokke-dô to the left and right and
a little to the front of the Fukû Kensaku Kannon *(Plate 52)*.
However, since they differ in size and material from the other statues
in the hall, it is considered doubtful that they were originally intended
for their present location.

The two statues are alike except that Nikkô wears a priest's robe
over his garment, while Gakkô does not. Iconographically, the two
resemble Brahma and Indra, and it has been conjectured that they
were originally intended to represent those deities. Whether this is
the case or not, the images represent technical perfection in clay
statuary. At first they were brightly colored, but the pigment has now
come off, exposing a priming of potter's clay mixed with mica dust.
The Gakkô is in better condition than its companion piece. Only
small portions of the ear lobes and the index fingers have been
restored, the figure as a whole being intact.

PLATE 54 SCULPTURE

NARA PERIOD [645—794]

SHÛKONGÔ-JIN (VAJRAPANI)
*Clay. Height: 173.2 cm. Placed in the Hokke-dô of the Tôdaiji,
Nara.*

Shûkongô-jin is one of the benevolent deities who protect Buddhism.
The image of him shown here stands in a black lacquer miniature
shrine, back to back with the Fukû Kensaku Kannon in the Hokke-dô
(Plate 52). Since the Muromachi period, this has been a "secret
Buddha" *(hibutsu),* on view only one day each year, and, as a result,
it is in comparatively good condition.

According to legend, Rôben, the priest who founded the Tôdaiji,
worshiped this statue before that great monastery was established.
If this is true, the image is older than the others now housed in the
Hokke-dô *(Plates 52 and 53),* and in fact, it does seem somewhat
earlier in style.

The statue portrays the deity as he is about to strike a tremendous
blow against evil. His club is poised in the air, and his mouth is open
in a loud cry. The upper half of his body is bent tautly forward, and
his waist drawn slightly to the right. The entire effect of the image
is one of overpowering strength.

154

PLATE 55 SCULPTURE

NARA PERIOD [645—794]

KÔMOKU-TEN (VIRUPAKSA)
One of the Four Deva Kings (Shi Tennô). Clay. Height: 162.7 cm. Placed in the Kaidan-dô (Hall of Ordination) of the Tôdaiji, Nara.

According to the archives of the Tôdaiji, the original Four Deva Kings in the Hall of Ordination were bronze statues. The present clay ones were probably brought here from some other building in the monastery, but their history is totally unknown. They are approximately of human size. Originally they were colored with cinnabar, red, brown, green, and blue pigment and further decorated with gold dust and strips of gold leaf. Now, however, the coloring has fallen off, leaving a surface finished in potter's clay mixed with powdered mica.

Kômoku holds a sutra scroll in his left hand and a writing brush in his right. His forehead is wrinkled, and his eyes, instead of being wide open in a menacing expression of wrath, as is usual with the Four Deva Kings, peer thoughtfully into the distance. His hands, ears, and portions of his sleeves have been restored.

The Deva Kings, along with the Buddhas of the sun and the moon enshrined in the same building *(Plate 53)*, are considered to represent the high point of Nara clay sculpture.

PLATE 56 SCULPTURE

NARA PERIOD [645—794]

THE PRIEST GANJIN
Dry-lacquer. Height: 80.5 cm. Placed in the Kaizan-dô (Founder's Hall) of the Tôshôdai-ji, Nara.

In the early Nara period there was as yet no priest in Japan qualified to conduct an ordination ceremony with proper rites, and the Chinese priest Chien-chên, better known by his Japanese name, Ganjin, was invited to come to Japan for that purpose. After repeated shipwrecks and other mishaps, during the course of which he lost his eyesight, he finally arrived in 753 with twenty-four followers. In 759 he founded the Tôshôdai-ji, and until his death in 764 he worked strenuously at propagating Buddhism in Japan.

This statue until recently was believed to be a papier-mâché work, but when it was repaired in 1935, pieces of paper affixed during an earlier repairing were removed, and it was found to have been made by the dry-lacquer method. It is composed of from three to six layers of hemp cloth cemented with lacquer, and the surface is finished with a mixture of lacquer, sawdust, and other materials. Inside the statue there was discovered a simple framework of wood, probably the result of repairs made after a fire in the Tempô era (1830–1843). We can reasonably assume that the image originally had an intricately constructed frame, as did other contemporary works of this type. The coloring remains fairly intact—light pink on the flesh, green on the underclothing, and red on the main garment, with a beautiful varicolored design on the *kasaya* (an outer robe worn by priests).

158

PLATE 57 SCULPTURE

HEIAN PERIOD [794—1185]

YAKUSHI NYORAI (BHAISAJYA-GURU)
Wood. Height: 170 cm. Placed in the main hall of the Jingo-ji,
Kyoto.

This image is considered to have been the original main icon of the
Jingan-ji, which is the present-day Jingo-ji, and therefore to date
from the Enryaku era (782–805), when that monastery was founded.

The whole statue, including a portion of the lotus pedestal, is
carved of a single piece of sandalwood. The corpulent body, the stern
expression of the face, the emphatic lines of the drapery, and over-all
austerity are features that distinguish this from statues of the Nara
period. The single-block sculpture of the early Heian period is seen
here at its best.

160

PLATE 58   SCULPTURE

HEIAN PERIOD [794—1185]

THE GODDESS NAKATSU-HIME
Wood.   Height: 36.6 cm.   Owner: Yakushi-ji, Nara.

During the Heian period the native Japanese religion, Shinto, though
by no means forgotten, became virtually an adjunct of Buddhism,
which was in every way a more highly developed religion. Conscious
efforts were made to syncretize the two faiths, and it came to be
widely held that the indigenous gods were local manifestations of the
Buddhas and Bodhisattvas. Hitherto there had been no icons in
Shinto, but now images of the native deities began to appear. The
one seen here is from a set of three thought to be the oldest in
existence. They are said to have been enshrined in the Hachiman
Shrine at the Yakushi-ji since its foundation in the Kampyô era
(889–897). Like typical Buddhist statues of that age, the Nakatsu-
hime was carved from a single block of wood, only the top of the
head and the bottom of the garment being made separately. The
image is in the form of a Heian noblewoman, but the modeling gives
an impression of rather unladylike massiveness and force, and the
total effect is somewhat like that of contemporary Buddhas. The
colors, as well as the figure itself, are in exceptionally good condition.

162

PLATE 59 SCULPTURE

HEIAN PERIOD [794—1185]

AMIDA NYORAI (AMITABHA)
*By Jôchô (d. 1057). Wood. Height: 295 cm. Placed in the Phoenix
Hall (Hô-ô-dô) of the Byôdô-in, Kyoto.*

This statue is a work from the mature years of Jôchô. It is typical of
the style most commonly used during the latter half of the Heian
period. Jôchô was the formulator of artistic rules that served as the
guide to most later Buddhist sculptors *(see text, pages 22 and 23).*

164

PLATE 60 SCULPTURE

HEIAN PERIOD [794—1185]

KICHIJÔ-TEN (MAHASRI)
Wood. Height: 90 cm. Owner: Jôruri-ji, Kyoto.

The annals of the Jôruri-ji mention this statue under the date 1212, but it may have been produced earlier. It was carved in segments from cypress wood in a fashion not ordinarily found before the Kamakura period, but the crown and other accessories were made not of gilt bronze, as was usual in that epoch, but of wood, in the Heian manner. The date of the work is therefore problematic, but in general appearance it follows the elaborately decorative style of the late Heian period *(Plate 6)*. Like the famous Nara painting of the same deity *(Plate 3)*, the image seems more secular than religious.

166

PLATE 61 SCULPTURE

KAMAKURA PERIOD [1185—1338]

MUCHAKU (ASANGA)
By Unkei (late twelfth century). Wood. Height: 188 cm. Placed in the North Octagonal Hall of the Kôfuku-ji, Nara.

Unkei, who carved the present statue, was the leading sculptor of the Kamakura period. Born in Nara, he was no doubt influenced by the realistic statues in the ancient temples there, and the school that he established discarded the somewhat insipid style of the Heian age in favor of one that more closely resembled that of Nara times. Although this image was made for a religious purpose and given the name of the famous Indian bonze Asanga, it might well be considered as simply the portrait of a Japanese priest—it is lifelike in every respect. The natural treatment of the clothing calls to mind the similar effect in clay statues of the Nara period, such as the Buddha of the moon in the Hokke-dô *(Plate 53)*.

168

PLATE 62 SCULPTURE

KAMAKURA PERIOD [1185—1338]

TENTÔ-KI

By Kôben (early thirteenth century). From a pair of lantern-bearing goblins. Wood. Height: 77.8 cm. Owner: Kôfuku-ji, Nara.

This image was made in 1215. Like most Kamakura works, it was carved in segments. The eyes and the right fang are crystal, while the armlets and bracelets are gilt bronze. The hair was painted directly upon the wood in fine black lines, and the body appears to have been painted with cinnabar, while the shoulder pieces and the skirt have remnants of green pigment. Most of the original coloring, however, has come off. The wooden pedestal is antique in shape, and may originally have been intended for another, older, statue. It shows traces of having been scorched by fire.

The body of this demon is an outstanding specimen of Kamakura-period realism. It fully justifies the fame of the sculptor, Kôben, who was the third son of Unkei.

PLATE 63 SCULPTURE

KAMAKURA PERIOD [1185—1338]

BASU SENNIN (VASU)
*By Tankei (1173–1256). From the Twenty-eight Attendants of the
Thousand-Armed Kannon (Nijû-hachi-bu-shû). Wood. Height:
155 cm. In the Sanjûsangen-dô of the Myôhô-in, Kyoto.*

This image of a scrawny old man engaged in devotions is another fine
example of Kamakura realism. The statue was originally colored, but
most of the pigment has come off. Actually, however, the loss rather
enhances the effect of the carving. The work was for a long time
ascribed to Unkei, but it is now thought to have been made by his
eldest son Tankei in 1254.

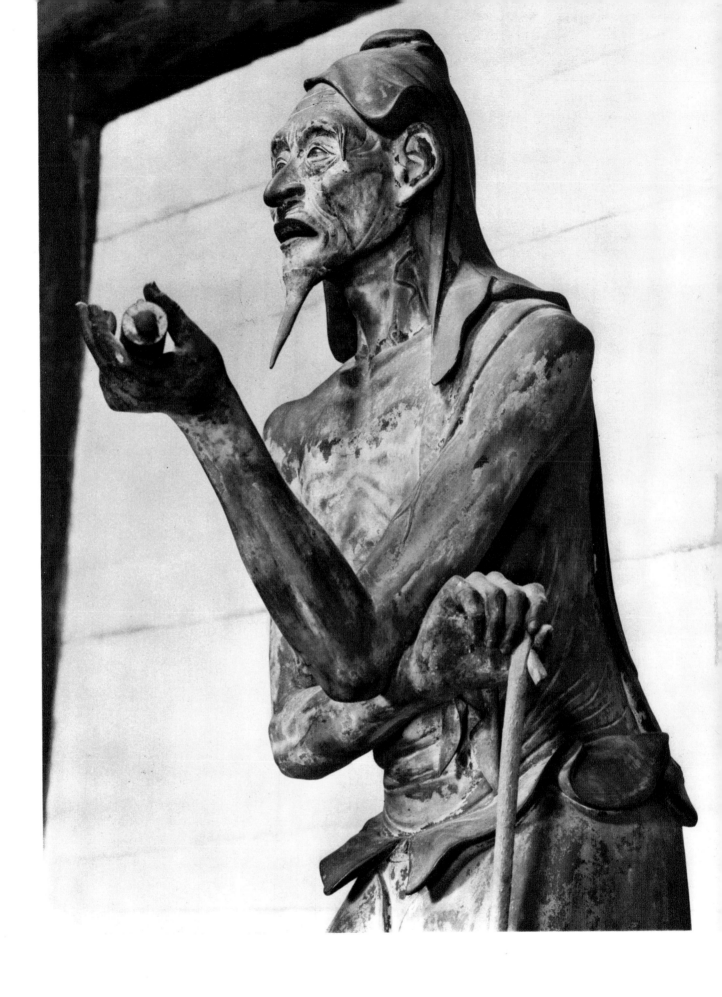

Plate 64 POTTERY

PREHISTORIC PERIOD [—552]

Jômon Pottery
Owner: Tokyo National Museum.

The name *jômon,* or "rope design," is given to pottery of this kind
because it is decorated with surface patterns made by applying coils
of rope. It is found at the lowest strata in archaeological sites and is
considered to represent the earliest culture in Japan. While it is
technically cruder than Yayoi vessels, which are found above it, it is
freer in form and on the whole more advanced artistically. The
earliest specimens are plain both in shape and in surface design, but
those of a somewhat later period are often exceedingly elaborate.

174

PLATE 65 POTTERY

NARA PERIOD [645—794]

JAR
Three-color glaze. Height: 15.7 cm. Diameter of mouth: 12.1 cm. Excavated at Ibaraki City, Osaka Prefecture. Owner: Tokyo National Museum.

This jar is reported to have been unearthed during the early years of Meiji (1868–1911) near the mausoleum of the Emperor Keitai, who is traditionally said to have reigned from 507 to 531. Its white, rather coarse-grained clay is similar to the material used for the tiles in temples erected during the Nara period. The outside is covered with yellow, green, and white glazes, and the inside with a pale green glaze. The partial change of the glaze to a silvery color is perhaps due to the jar's having been buried so long in the ground. The technique of glazing used here was imported from T'ang China, and is found in a number of examples in the Shôsô-in.

PLATE 67   POTTERY

MOMOYAMA PERIOD [1573—1615]

TEA BOWL

*Raku ware.   Known as "Fuji-san."   By Hon'ami Kôetsu (1558–1637).
Height: 8.5 cm.   Diameter of mouth: 11.5 cm.   Diameter of foot:
5.4 cm.   Owner: Mr. Tadamasa Sakai, Tokyo.*

Raku ware was originated by a certain Chôjirô, who is supposed to
have been the son of a Korean or Chinese immigrant. It was brought
to technical perfection by Chôjirô's grandson Donyû and given its
final artistic form by the renowned art connoisseur Hon'ami Kôetsu.
Kôetsu was a sword-maker by profession, but he was also a distinguished calligraphist, lacquer-worker, and potter. His ceramic
works have an air of nobility not found in those of the professional
raku potters. The vessel reproduced here, which he named "Fuji-san,"
or "Mt. Fuji," is, like that famous peak, considered peerless by the
Japanese.

180

PLATE 68 POTTERY

EDO PERIOD [1615—1867]

VASE
*Iga ware. Height: 28.0 cm. Diameter of mouth: 10.0 cm. Diameter
of foot: 12.0 cm. Owner: Nezu Museum, Tokyo.*

Iga Province (in present Mie Prefecture) in the early Momoyama
period was governed by the Tsutsui family, but towards the close of
the period it became the fief of the Tôdô family. Under Tsutsui rule
the Iga kilns produced mostly crude pottery for the use of the
farming populace, but in the time of the Tôdô they turned out many
fine tea-ceremony vessels. The one illustrated here is one of the best
of the existing Tôdô Iga vases. The biscuit, which is ash-gray, has been
fired to the hardness of stone, and the entire surface is covered with
a pale green glaze called the "glass" glaze of Iga. Variations in shade
result from high-temperature baking.

182

PLATE 69 PORCELAIN

EDO PERIOD [1615—1867]

VASE
Kakiemon-type. Height: 30.0 cm. Diameter of mouth: 6.3 cm. Diameter of foot: 10.9 cm. From a private collection.

Sakaida Kakiemon, a potter active in the first half of the seventeenth century at Arita in Hizen Province (present Saga Prefecture), was the first Japanese to succeed in making porcelain with overglaze color designs. His genuine works are all but impossible to identify, since his direct descendants used not only his technique, but his name as well, and since many other ceramists imitated his style. Works after the Kakiemon manner that are not definitely known to be by one of the Kakiemons, are generally described as "Kakiemon-type" (*Kakiemon-de*).

Kakiemon-type wares fall into two categories, those decorated with overglaze colors alone, and those having a blue underglaze as well. The present example is, of course, of the former class. It is a rare example of Kakiemon ware in the shape of a bottle.

184

PLATE 70   PORCELAIN

EDO PERIOD [1615—1867]

DISH
*Imari porcelain.   Height: 6.1 cm.   Diameter of mouth: 32.7 cm.
Diameter of base: 17.0 cm.   Owner: Tokyo National Museum.*

The colorful dish shown here is typical of Imari ware, which was
an outgrowth of the style created by Kakiemon. The brushwork
displayed in the design is very painstaking, and the carelessness often
found in Imari ware is absent. The treatment of the blossoms and
wisteria vines, however, is free and natural. The two women, one
carrying a bird-cage and the other dancing with a fan in hand,
remind one of the women drawn by the famous color-print artist
Hishikawa Moronobu *(Plate 37)*. Their hairdress is in a style that was
popular in the Genroku era (1688–1703), and it is likely that the
dish was produced at about that time.

PLATE 71 PORCELAIN

EDO PERIOD [1615—1867]

DISH

Old Kutani porcelain. Height: 4.0 cm. Diameter of mouth: 35.0 cm. Diameter of base: 19.0 cm. Owner: Tokyo National Museum.

On the inside of this large dish a design of peonies has been painted in purple, green, yellow, and red, while on the outside there is an arabesque in cobalt blue. The dull-white clay of the base, as well as the deep green and purple glazes, are typical of early Kutani porcelain which is spoken of technically as "Old Kutani" to distinguish it from modern products of the Kutani kilns. Kutani has some qualities in common with the porcelain of Ming China, but it is closer in spirit to the sumptuousness of Momoyama paintings than to the prettiness so often found in Chinese wares.

71

PLATE 72 PORCELAIN

EDO PERIOD [1615—1867]

JAR
*By Nonomura Ninsei (seventeenth century).   Height: 27.7 cm.
Diameter of mouth: 10.3 cm.   Owner: Seika-dô Foundation, Tokyo.*

Ninsei was one of a number of expert potters who worked in Kyoto during the Edo period. The dates of his birth and death are unknown, but he was active during the last decades of the seventeenth century. He is known particularly for his multicolored designs, which with their gold and silver figures call to mind the gorgeous decorative paintings of the Momoyama period.

The jar shown here was intended as a tea container. Its base of yellowish clay is coated with a translucent white glaze, over which there is a design of cherry trees in bloom. Some of the blossoms are red with gold outlines, while others are silver with red outlines. The gold cloud-like design at the top has spots of green and indigo here and there, while the background is jet black. In general, the effect is somewhat like that of ornate lacquer ware, as is the case with many of Ninsei's other works.

PLATE 73 PORCELAIN

EDO PERIOD [1615—1867]

BOWL

By Nin'ami Dôhachi (1783–1855). Design of cherry blossoms and maple trees. Height: 8.8 cm. Diameter: 18.2 cm. Diameter of base: 7.6 cm. From a private collection.

The clay base of this bowl is coated with a transparent, faintly blue glaze, and over the glaze, on both the inside and the outside are painted cherry trees in full bloom and maples with resplendent scarlet leaves. The trunks of the cherry trees are done in dark brown, the blossoms in white, and the maple leaves in red and green. Gold is added in several places to complete the lavish color scheme. This design follows the Sôtatsu-Kôrin style of decorative painting, which was adopted into ceramic art by Kôrin's brother, Ogata Kenzan, at about the close of the Genroku era (1688–1703).

PLATE 74 TEXTILES

ASUKA PERIOD [552—645]

KANTÔ BROCADE
Actual size. Owner: Tokyo National Museum.

"Kantô" as applied to this fabric is written with the same characters as those for the Chinese province of Kwangtung, but the choice of characters may have little or nothing to do with the real significance of the word, which is uncertain. The same term is used to refer to a weave that was introduced from China in the Muromachi period, but in this case different ideographs are ordinarily employed. Whatever the true derivation of the word, the fabric shown here is one of the oldest in Japan. It belongs to a collection of treasures preserved in the Hôryû-ji, but presented by that monastery to the imperial household at the beginning of the Meiji era (1868–1911) and now in the custody of the Tokyo National Museum. A number of similar fragments are found in the Shôsô-in.

The design was made by the *kasuri* method; that is to say, it was woven of threads that had previously been dyed in segments so as to produce the desired pattern. It is not, therefore, a brocade in the usual sense, but then the Japanese word for brocade seems in pre-modern times to have been used generally for cloth with varicolored woven designs.

No fabrics produced by the *kasuri* method have been found among ancient Chinese or Korean remains, nor is there anything in the historical documents of China and Korea that suggests it. There are, however, several weaves of this type in the South Sea Islands, notably around Sumatra, and it is possible that the technique or the material itself came to Japan from that region.

194

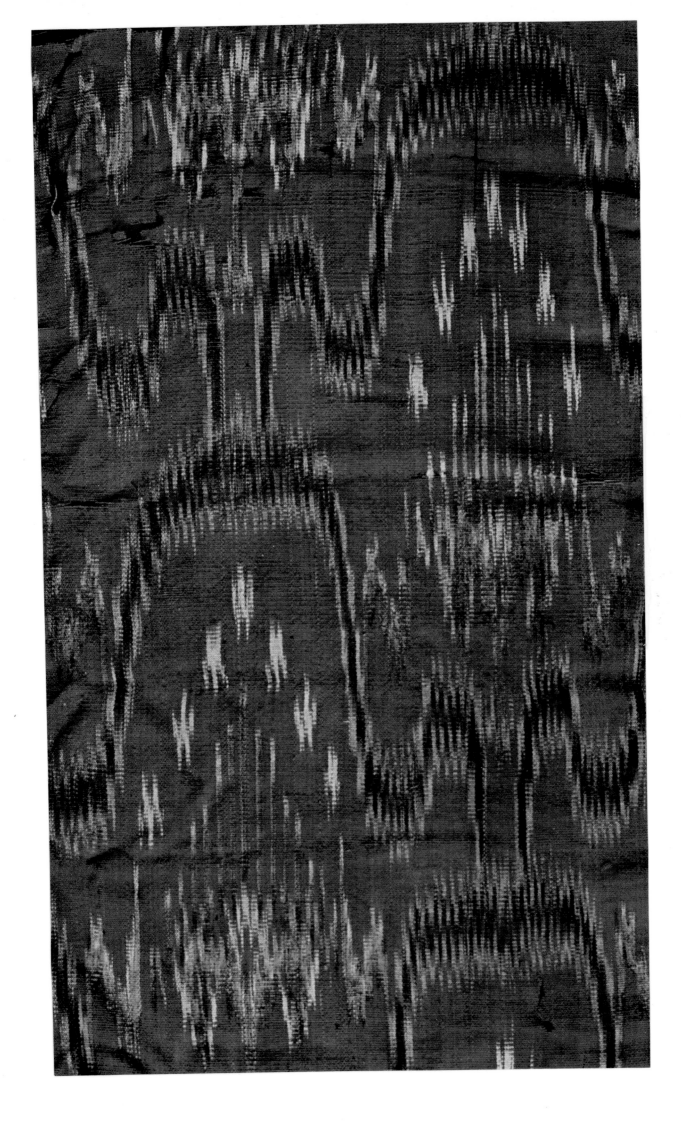

PLATE 75 TEXTILES

NARA PERIOD [645—794]

BROCADE
Actual size. Owner: Tokyo National Museum.

This brocade is particularly famous among the Nara fabrics preserved in the Shôsô-in. It has customarily been called the cover of a lute, since a large fragment is cut in the shape of that instrument, but small pieces seem to have been used in various ways, and the present cut is made up into a cushion with a red felt filling. The cloth is composed of colored weft threads in about nine shades, including green, red, white, purple, and yellow, woven on a sapphire-blue base. The design was magnificent in scale, the complete unit being nearly three feet square. The part seen here is the central floral pattern. It was surrounded by a wreath of small blossoms.

To weave a brocade of this sort, a draw loom was used. An assistant stood at the top of it and, coordinating his movements with those of the weaver, picked up the warp threads as needed. On a modern Jacquard loom, several tens of thousands of perforated pattern cards would probably be necessary to make the design shown here. The imagination is staggered by the thought of the time and effort that must have been required to produce it by hand.

PLATE 76 TEXTILES

EDO PERIOD [1615—1867]

Kosode (detail)
Length: 148 cm. Owner: Nagao Museum of Art, Tokyo.

This fabric is of a type fashionable in the Momoyama and Edo periods.
On the upper half of the flaming red satin section, a long-tailed bird
is seen flying among blossom-laden cherry branches, while in the
lower half a mandarin duck plays among the waves of a lake. The
embroidery is in red, white, violet, green, and other colors, and
glittering gold foil is affixed in places. This cloth probably dates from
the Kyôhô era (1716–1735), when Edo textiles were in every sense
at their peak. The kimono of which this is a part was intended for
the Noh theater. Although Noh costumes in general had become more
and more sumptuous since the beginning of the Edo period, few others
from that age compare in splendor with this,

PLATE 77   TEXTILES

EDO   PERIOD   [1615—1867]

Noh Costume *(Atsuita Karaori)*
Length: 151.6 cm.   Owner: Tokyo National Museum.

The *karaori* (literally, "Chinese weave") is the most colorful and
luxurious of Noh costumes. It is usually worn as an outer garment by
actors in female roles. The *atsuita,* which is the basic men's costume,
frequently has a design in large squares or in latticework. The *atsuita
karaori* is simply an *atsuita* woven in the brilliant *karaori* style. It can
be used both as the principal kimono, like the *atsuita,* or as an outer
garment, like the *karaori.*

The Noh was originally connected with religion, and it developed
under the patronage of the shogun and the feudal lords. It is not,
therefore, surprising that the majority of costumes used in this drama
are very expensive and elegant. The tendency during the Edo period
was for them to grow even more so.

In the present kimono there is, on the white and green squares,
a cobblestone pattern woven with gold thread. In addition there is
an over-all lattice pattern woven in colored thread, and on this are
scattered paper-mulberry leaves in various colors. In early times it was
said that if one wrote a wish on a paper-mulberry leaf during the
Tanabata festival, the wish would come true. Because of this tradition,
this leaf was frequently used as a pattern on clothing and various
other articles.

200

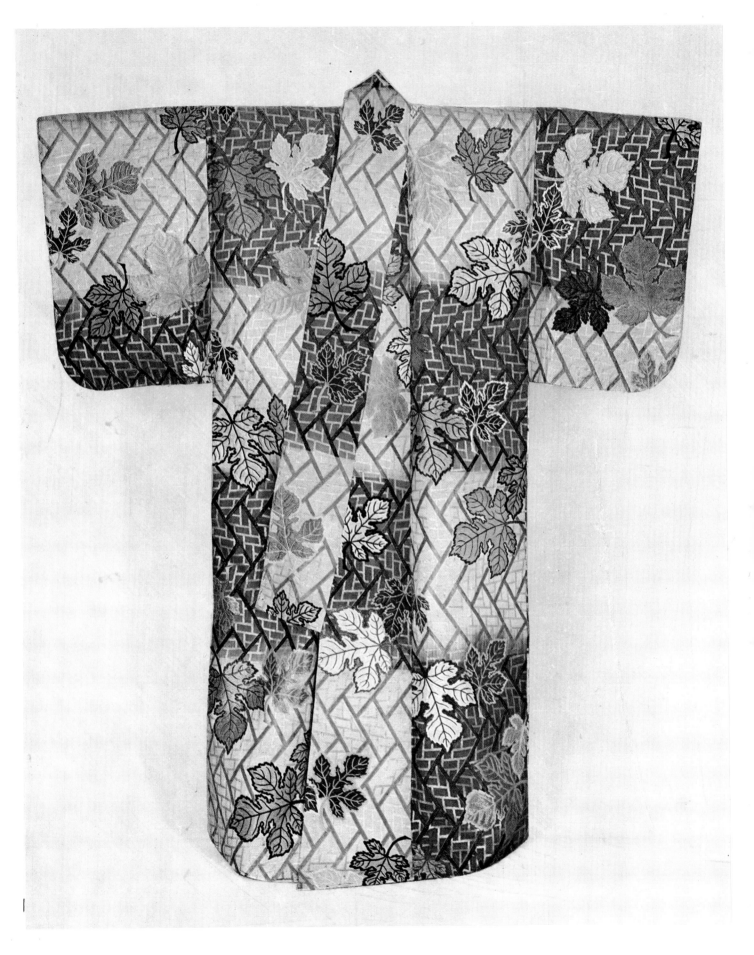

PLATE 78 TEXTILES

EDO PERIOD [1615—1867]

KIMONO *(detail)*
Dyed by the Yûzen method.   160 cm.   Owner: Nagao Museum of
Art, Kanagawa Prefecture.

By the Yûzen method large pictorial designs were drawn in dye on
a fabric with an implement resembling a toothpick, and then the cloth
was dyed by means of a rice-paste resist. The technique appears to have
been developed by a painter named Miyazaki Yûzensai, who was
active in Kyoto during the Genroku era (1688–1703), but facts
concerning this artist's life and the origin of his process are obscure.
Yûzen designs, which are much bolder and freer than the tie-dyed
patterns of earlier times, became exceedingly popular during the Edo
period and have remained so until today. The picture on the fabric
shown here shows a group of houses and shops in the famous
Yoshiwara district of Edo. The buildings are drawn in perspective,
and great care has been taken to show every detail. The effect is
very much like that of contemporaneous woodblock prints.

202

PLATE 79   LACQUER WARE

HEIAN PERIOD [794—1185]

COSMETICS BOX
Maki-e.   *22.5×30.3×13 cm.   Owner: The Committee for the Preservation of Cultural Properties, Tokyo.*

The graceful design on this box shows wheels floating in a quiet stream. It was probably suggested by the practice of putting wheels in water to prevent them from drying out, and it is also found on mirror-backs and other objects from the late Heian period. The arrangement of the wheel segments here is extremely skillful. Though seemingly scattered in artless fashion, they are nevertheless in perfect balance. Pure gold and gold mixed with silver are used alternately on the lines in the wheels, while occasional bits of mother-of-pearl inlay add color and serve the function of drawing the design together. The inside of the box is decorated with figures of butterflies, birds, and flowers.

204

PLATE 80 LACQUER WARE

MOMOYAMA PERIOD [1573—1615]

TRAY
Diameter: 36 cm. Owner: Mr. Tomio Yoshino, Tokyo.

Lacquer painting in red, yellow, and green, which is illustrated here,
is made by a method dating back to ancient times in China. It had
already developed to a high level by the former Han dynasty (206
B.C.–9 A.D.) as can be seen from artifacts found at Lok-lang, in
Korea. The pictorial decoration of the Tamamushi Shrine in the
Hôryû-ji, which is the oldest example of Japanese painting, was done
by this method. After its early appearance, however, it fell into
neglect, not to be revived until the Momoyama period. Since then
it has enjoyed continued favor.

206

PLATE 81 LACQUER WARE

EDO PERIOD [1615—1867]

Ink-Stone Box
*By Ogata Kôrin (1658–1716). Maki-e. 28×20×14.5 cm. Owner:
Tokyo National Museum.*

Although the *maki-e* displayed much brilliance in the late Momoyama
and early Edo periods, after the Genroku era (1688–1703) it fell
victim to a general trend toward empty virtuosity. The imaginative
works of Ogata Kôrin, however, are exceptions to the rule. Kôrin is
known particularly for preserving the tradition of Kôetsu and Sôtatsu
in painting, but, like Kôetsu, he tried his hand in several different
fields. The *maki-e* shown here is one of his masterpieces. The design
of a bridge and irises, which covers the entire surface, is based on the
section in the *Tales of Ise (Ise Monogatari)* that deals with the
Yatsuhashi district in Mikawa Province (present Aichi Prefecture).
Yatsuhashi derives its name, which means literally "eightfold bridge,"
from its most famous landmark, a bridge consisting of eight stone
sections set at irregular angles to each other. The design shows the
bridge in lead, the supporting posts in silver, the iris blossoms in inlaid
shell, and the stalks of the irises in gold. The entire surface is unified
by the rambling bridge, and the over-all composition is splendid.

208

PLATE 82 METALWORK

MUROMACHI PERIOD [1338—1573]

KETTLE FOR THE TEA CEREMONY
Ashiya type. Iron, with relief. Height: 19.0 cm. Diameter of body: 27.4 cm. Owner: Tokyo National Museum.

With the spread of the tea cult in the Muromachi, simple iron kettles came into demand for use in the tea ceremony. The best were made at Ashiya, a seaside village near the present River Onga in Fukuoka Prefecture. Among the earlier Ashiya kettles the one shown here, which probably dates from the mid-fifteenth century, is outstanding. Made of cast iron, it has a relief design of five lively horses, two on the front and three on the back, while on its shoulder appear the contours of distant hills. The kettle is of the orthodox type used in the tea ceremony. It is said to have once belonged to Furuta Oribe Masashige, a celebrated tea master and potter of the Momoyama period.

PLATE 83   METALWORK

MUROMACHI PERIOD [1338—1573]

SUTRA BOX
Bronze, gilded, with openwork.   Height: 10.2 cm.   Length: 30.3 cm.
Width: 18.8 cm.   Owner: Yôhô-ji, Kyoto.

This beautiful container has been preserved in the Yôhô-ji as an
article of daily use. The lid and body were shaped by hammering,
and all surfaces except the bottom are decorated with an openwork
arabesque of lotuses, while the edges of the figures in the design are
embellished with chiseled lines. The whole box is plated with gold.
On the bottom there appears an inscription bearing the date Temmon
24 (1555).

The metalwork of the Muromachi period shows unmistakable
symptoms of decline, but the present box is an exception. The lotus
design is executed with marvelous skill, and the shape of the box
matches it in beauty. All in all, this is a fine example of the delicacy
and technical perfection achieved by medieval Japanese metalworkers.

PLATE 84 ARCHITECTURE

PREHISTORIC PERIOD [—552]

HANIWA HOUSE
Terra cotta. Plan: 60×65 cm. Height: 53 cm. Excavated from an ancient burial mound at Saitobaru, Koyu-gun, Miyazaki Prefecture. Owner: Tokyo National Museum.

There are no existing specimens of the houses in which the ancient Japanese lived, but their general structure can be conjectured from the *haniwa* houses, from designs on bronze bells *(dôtaku)* and mirrors, and from the actual appearance of a few Shinto shrines that retain their original form.

It is uncertain whether the model shown here represented a single building or a group of buildings. In either case, however, it reveals much concerning the roof and other architectural elements of prehistoric dwellings.

214

PLATE 85 ARCHITECTURE

ASUKA PERIOD [552—645]

THE MAIN HALL OF THE HÔRYÛ-JI
13.9×10.7 m.   Located at Ikaruga-machi, Ikoma-gun, Nara Prefecture.

In 587 the Emperor Yômei fell seriously ill, and, thinking to secure his recovery by religious means, he ordered his consort, later the Empress Suiko, and his son, Prince Shôtoku, to build a temple and enshrine therein a statue of Yakushi, the Buddha of Medicine. The emperor died before the work was finished, but the empress and the prince completed the temple in the hope of adding to his good fortune in the afterlife. In this way the Hôryû-ji was established.

It has long been a subject of heated discussion whether the main hall of this monastery is the original one or a reconstruction made after a fire that is recorded to have destroyed the original in 670. It is generally agreed, however, that in either case the building is in the style of the Asuka period. In floor plan it is almost square, the upper story being considerably smaller than the lower. The railings, eave-support brackets, and other architectural devices are very much like details found in the Chinese rock-cave temples of Yün-kang and Lung-mên, which were made in the fifth and sixth centuries.

The interior of the building was destroyed by fire in 1949, but has recently been rebuilt.

216

PLATE 86   ARCHITECTURE

ASUKA PERIOD [552—645]

THE FIVE-STORIED PAGODA OF THE HÔRYÛ-JI
Base: 6.4 m. square.   Height: 31.9 m.   Located at Ikaruga-machi, Ikoma-gun, Nara Prefecture.

The tower of the Hôryû-ji, built some thirteen centuries ago, is still one of the most beautiful buildings of its type in Japan. In architectural detail it is similar to the main hall of the same monastery, the two constituting together a double monument to the ingenuity of Asuka architects.

The typical monastery of the Asuka period was enclosed by earthen walls with a main entrance on the south side. Inside there was a smaller gate that led into a rectangular court surrounded by corridors and containing the main hall and pagoda. Behind these and directly north of the two gates there was a lecture hall, in the sides of which the corridors terminated. Around the central compound stood priests' dormitories, a bell tower, sutra repositories, and a refectory, arranged in one of several ways. There were two systems for the placement of the pagoda and the main hall, the two most important buildings. One was that of the Hôryû-ji, in which they stood side by side on a line roughly perpendicular to the north-south axis. The other was that of the Shi-Tennô-ji, another monastery built by Prince Shôtoku, in which they lay one behind the other on the axis itself. Precedents for the latter plan have been discovered in China, but the Hôryû-ji system appears to have been original. How widely it was used is uncertain, nor is there any way of knowing whether its over-all artistic effect was as pleasing in other monasteries as in the Hôryû-ji. Certainly, as seen there, the low, bulky main hall and the soaring pagoda balance each other beautifully, although they are arranged asymmetrically.

218

PLATE 87 ARCHITECTURE

NARA PERIOD [645—794]

THE EASTERN PAGODA OF THE YAKUSHI-JI
Base: 7.9 m. square.   Height: 33.9 m.   Located at Nishinokyô-machi,
Nara Prefecture.

The Yakushi-ji was founded by the Emperor Temmu (reigned 673–686), and the building shown here is thought to date, in style at least, from the reign of the succeeding Empress Jitô (686–697). The monastery was moved to Nara in 710, but was rebuilt in its original form. The arrangement of its buildings represented a transition from Asuka architecture to that of the mature Nara period. As in later examples, the plan called for two identical pagodas, of which this is one. However, they were enclosed within the central compound in the Asuka fashion instead of being placed between the compound and the outer earthern wall, as was the case in Nara monasteries.

The Eastern Pagoda is the only one of the reconstructions of 710 still standing and the sole existing specimen of early Nara architecture. Although it has only three stories, it is one of the highest pagodas in Japan. The space between stories is broken by auxiliary eaves, an embellishment that has always been favored by Japanese architects. The bracketing under the eaves is lighter, though more complex, than in the Hôryû-ji pagoda, and the structure as a whole is more graceful.

220

PLATE 88 ARCHITECTURE

NARA PERIOD [645—794]

THE MAIN HALL OF THE TÔSHÔDAI-JI
27.9×14.5 m. Located at Gojô-machi, Nara.

The Tôshôdai-ji was founded in 759 by the priest Ganjin *(Plate 56)*. It is considered to have been only slightly smaller than the great official monasteries established during the Nara period. Its main hall, shown here, is the only large-scale structure of its type that has survived from that age. Low and oblong, this building shows a marvelous sense of proportion on the part of the architect. Its roof formerly sloped even more gently than now.

222

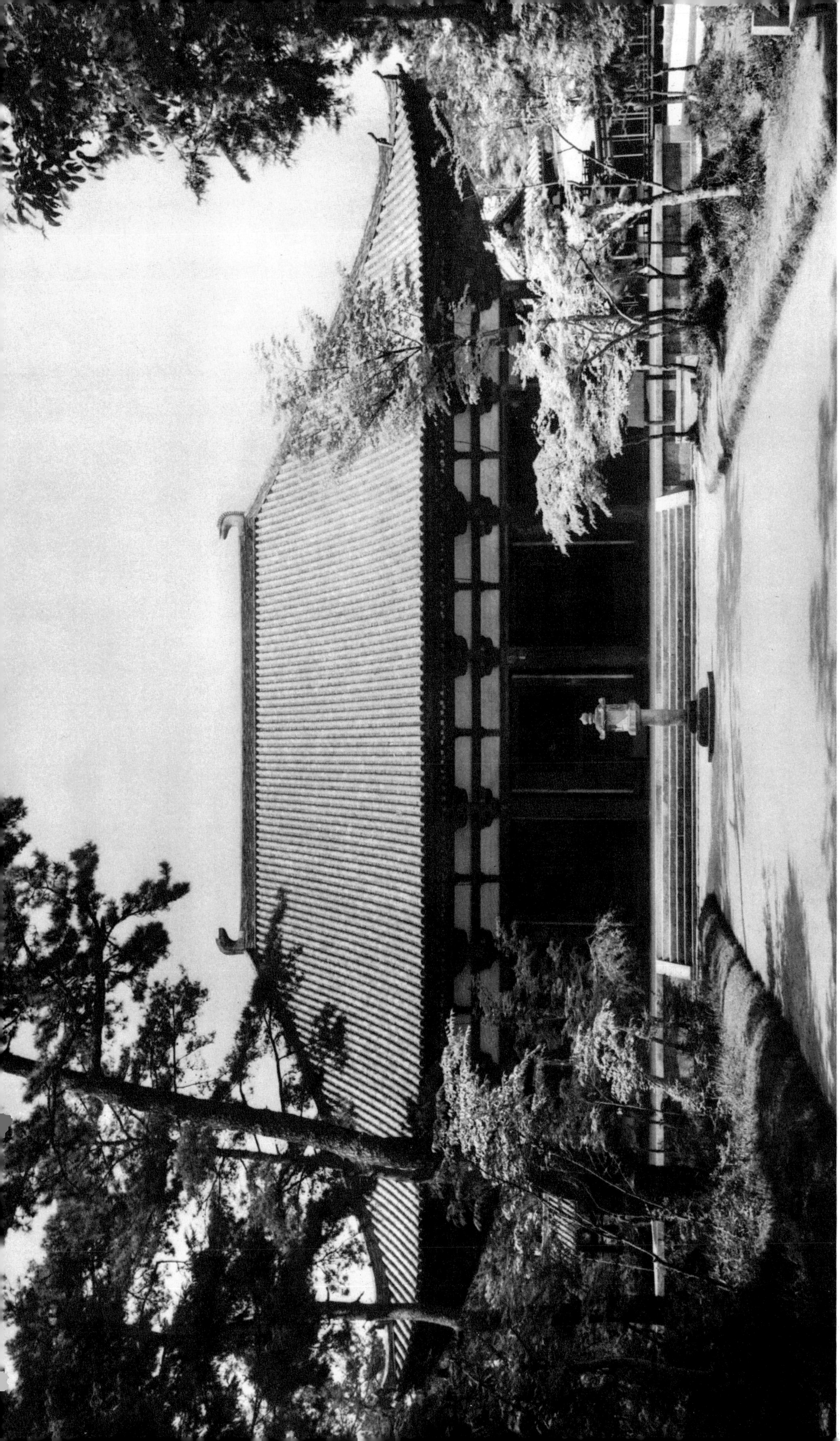

PLATE 89 ARCHITECTURE

NARA PERIOD [645—794]

THE YUME-DONO OF THE HÔRYÛ-JI
*Octagonal.   Diameter (between sides): 4.8 m.   Height: 12.8 m.
Located at Ikaruga-machi, Ikoma-gun, Nara Prefecture.*

During the Tempyô era (729–749), the priest Gyôshin, deploring the
state of ruin into which the Ikaruga Palace of Prince Shôtoku had
fallen, resolved to create in its place an area sacred to the prince's
memory. The outcome of his resolution was the Eastern Precinct of
the Hôryû-ji. The octagonal building shown here is the central
structure in the compound. It is usually known as the Yume-dono, or
"Hall of Visions," because of a legend that the prince, while con-
templating Buddhist teachings, had envisioned the Buddha in the
building that had originally stood on this site.

Portions of the Yume-dono were altered in the course of repairs
made during the Kamakura period, but the structure retains its
original grace and dignity. Even today it is the finest of all Japanese
octagonal buildings.

224

PLATE 90   ARCHITECTURE

HEIAN PERIOD [794—1185]

THE PHOENIX HALL OF THE BYÔDÔ-IN
*Central hall: 10.3×7.9 m.   Left and right corridors: 19.2×3.9 m.
Left and right towers: 3.1 m. square and 11 m. high.   Rear corridor:
15.9×4.2 cm.   Located at Uji-shi, Kyoto Prefecture.*

When the regent Fujiwara Yorimichi took the tonsure in 1052, he
constructed a magnificent monastery on his estate at Uji. In the
following year the building shown here was erected therein to house
an image of the Buddha Amida (Amitabha). The central hall is
typical of the many temples dedicated to that Buddha by the Heian
nobility. Its basic structure is only three bays by two, but the broad
hipped-and-gabled roof and the auxiliary eaves beneath it give an
impression of greater size. Inside there is an ornate sanctum one bay
square, in which is enshrined the central icon.

The corridors and annexes are thought to bear considerable
resemblance to the *shinden* style of palace architecture. This combination of religious and secular styles is symbolic of the worldly attitude
toward religion that prevailed among the aristocrats of the age.
Yorimichi and his fellow noblemen tried, by building palatial temples
of this sort, to create replicas of the infinite and everlasting paradise of
Amida—vanity, perhaps, but at the same time a reflection of the
integral part that religion played in their everyday lives.

226

PLATE 91 ARCHITECTURE

HEIAN PERIOD [794—1185]

The Nageire-dô of the Sambutsu-ji
Main structure: 3.9×2.4 m. Corridors on two sides: 1.5 m. wide.
Located at Mitoku-mura, Tôbaku-gun, Tottori Prefecture.

The Sambutsu-ji atop Mt. Mitoku is one of the secluded mountain
monasteries of esoteric Buddhism. Its Nageire-dô, or literally,
"Throwing-in Hall," is a tiny building perched on the side of a cliff
and approached by way of a cave. The main structure is only one
bay square, but it is enlarged on two sides with separately covered
corridors. The unconventional plan of the building is in good keeping
with its seemingly precarious situation.

Small detached halls were numerous in esoteric Buddhist establishments, and many of them, like the one shown here, display the
harmony of man-made structure with natural surroundings that so
appeals to the Japanese aesthetic sense.

Plate 92 Architecture

KAMAKURA PERIOD [1185—1338]

The Pagoda of the Ishiyama-dera
Base: 5.8 m. square. Height: 16.1 m. Located at Ishiyama Terabe-machi, Ōtsu, Shiga Prefecture.

Pagodas of the type shown here are associated with Shingon Buddhism, and were introduced to Japan together with that sect in the early Heian period. No example from that age has survived, but this building, which dates from 1194, is supposed to have been modeled after a Heian pattern.

The form derives from the hemispherical stupas of India, but the addition of pent-roofs to the lower portions has all but completely hidden the basic round structure. The upper portion has also been expanded and sinicized, so that the general appearance is that of a two-storied pagoda, of which the lower floor is square and the upper circular.

230

PLATE 93   ARCHITECTURE

KAMAKURA   PERIOD   [1185—1338]

THE RELIQUARY HALL OF THE ENGAKU-JI
*Base: 8.2 m. square.   Located at Yamanouchi, Ôfuna-machi, Kama-
kura, Kanagawa Prefecture.*

The Engaku-ji, which was constructed at the behest of Hôjô Tokimune
(1251–1284) around 1282, was one of the five great monasteries of
Kamakura, famous as centers of Zen art and letters. The building
shown here was erected during the Einin era (1293–1298) and is the
only one of the original buildings in the five compounds that still
stands. It is the classic example of what is known as the "Chinese
style" *(kara-yô),* which was introduced during the Kamakura period,
and which was later employed generally for Zen temples. This style
is characterized by simplicity and lightness of structure. Curved lines,
such as those seen here in the roof and the windows, are prominent.
Eave-support brackets, which are of a distinctive shape, are employed
not only above columns, as is usual in other modes, but in the space
between them as well. The rafters are arranged in fan style at the
corners, making possible a pronounced upward curve in the eaves.
Each of these features was frequently employed in the combination-
style buildings of the Muromachi and subsequent periods.

232

PLATE 94 ARCHITECTURE

MUROMACHI PERIOD [1338—1573]

THE MAIN HALL OF THE KANSHIN-JI
*Base: 19.4×17.7 m. Located at Kawakami-mura, Minami Kôchi-gun,
Osaka.*

It is traditionally said that the Kanshin-ji was founded in 836, but
its present main hall, which is shown here, was built in about 1375.
It is seven bays square in size, the front portion, two bays in depth,
being the outer sanctum and the remainder, the inner sanctum. This
form is characteristic of Shingon temples.

The woodwork supporting the eaves is chiefly in the "Japanese
style," but the absence of the middle block on the brackets is typical
of the "Indian style," and various other details are in the "Chinese
style." All in all, this building is one of the best existing specimens of
the eclectic style that developed during the Kamakura and Muromachi periods. Many later temples are built along the same lines.

234

PLATE 95   ARCHITECTURE

MUROMACHI PERIOD [1338—1573]

THE SILVER PAVILION (GINKAKU)
First story: 7.9×5.9 m.   Located at Ginkaku-ji-machi, Sakyô-ku, Kyoto.

The building shown here was built by the eighth Ashikaga Shogun Yoshimasa (1435–1490) in 1480 as a part of a villa on the outskirts of Kyoto. It is modeled in general on the Golden Pavilion (Kinkaku), built by Yoshimasa's grandfather Yoshimitsu (1385–1408), but it is considerably smaller than the earlier building and differs from it in a number of stylistic details.

The first story is in the *shinden* style of residential architecture, except that it has sliding doors instead of folding shutters. The second floor follows the lines of the "Chinese style" used in contemporary Zen monasteries. It is said that Yoshimasa proposed to cover the upper floor inside and out with silver, but died before his plan was realized. Notwithstanding this, the building is commonly known today as the Ginkaku, or "Silver Pavilion." It is one of the most important examples of residential architecture in the Muromachi period.

236

PLATE 96 ARCHITECTURE

MUROMACHI PERIOD [1338—1573]

GARDEN OF THE RYÔAN-JI
Located at Goryô-no-shita-machi, Ukyô-ku, Kyoto.

The Ryôan-ji was originally the villa of the military lord Hosokawa Katsumoto (1430–1473). It was converted into a Zen monastery during the Bummei era (1469–1486), and the present garden was probably laid out in about 1500. It is traditionally said to have been designed by Sôami (d. 1525), an artist in the service of the shogunate, but there is little documentary evidence for the tradition.

The garden is very small, occupying only about one tenth of an acre. Made entirely of sand and rocks, it is at once simple and abstruse, like the subtle ink monochromes produced by contemporary Zen priest-painters. To some it suggests islands in the ocean, to others, mountain peaks soaring above an expanse of clouds, and to still others, a variety of different scenes or ideas. The underlying spirit is that of Zen Buddhism. As the Zen believer seeks ultimate truth by clearing his mind of ephemeral thoughts, the artist has tried by discarding unessentials to reveal the inner soul of nature.

238

PLATE 97 ARCHITECTURE

MOMOYAMA PERIOD [1573—1615]

The Himeji Castle
Located at Himeji, Hyôgo Prefecture.

Castles of the kind shown here appeared during the very late Muromachi period. Despite their having a number of features alien to ordinary Japanese architecture—in particular the prominent whitewashed walls—they are not considered to be of foreign origin by Japanese scholars, who instead think them to have developed from a form of one-story watchtower used in Muromachi-period fortresses. The Himeji Castle, completed during the Keichô era (1596–1614), is the most beautiful example still standing.

Within strongholds like this, feudal lords built magnificent palaces, whose walls and doors, like those of the castles themselves, were covered with gorgeous paintings on gold and silver backgrounds. It was to decorate the cavernous rooms of such buildings that Eitoku, Tôhaku, and their confrères created the bold style of painting for which they are famous (*see Plates 27 and 28*).

PLATE 98 ARCHITECTURE

EDO PERIOD [1615—1867]

GARDEN AND SHÔKIN-TEI TEAHOUSE OF THE KATSURA PALACE
Located at Katsura, Ukyô-ku, Kyoto.

The Katsura Detached Palace was built between 1620 and 1624 by
Prince Tomohito, the younger brother of the Emperor Go-Yôzei
(reigned 1586–1610), and later enlarged by Tomohito's son Tomotada.
The Shôkin-tei, or "Pine-lute Pavilion," which is shown here, is one
of the oldest and most beautiful buildings in the compound. Its name
is said to have been chosen because the sound of the wind through
the nearby pines is like the music of a lute. The building is little more
than a rustic cottage, but it manifests the best features of Japanese
domestic architecture. In it, the plainest of materials are used in such
a way as to give miraculous variety in shape and line. This is
particularly true in the case of the dirt-floor veranda *(Plate 99),*
which functions as a link between the interior of the house and the
garden.

Gardens of the Edo period fell into two classes. One was the
miniature teahouse garden, in which an effort was made by clever
use of a few plants and rocks to persuade the viewer for a moment
that he was in a quiet, still place deep in the mountains. The other
type was the large "tour garden," such as the one shown here, which
was designed for quiet strolls. Gardens of this sort were an outgrowth of
the *shinden* style, with its miniature landscapes, but they also show the
influence of Zen Buddhism and the tea ceremony. As one proceeds
from house to house in the Katsura garden, one is presented with
a series of beautifully arranged scenes which were inspired by the
Tale of Genji and other literary classics, but which have to some
extent the same symbolic effect as ink landscape paintings.

The gardens of the Edo period were not as a rule so austere as
earlier ones associated with Zen. They aimed not at conveying a lofty
idea, but simply at giving a glimpse of nature at its best. In other
words, they were the products of an instinctive love of nature rather
than a philosophical concept of it.

242

PLATE 99   ARCHITECTURE
EDO PERIOD [1615—1867]

Veranda of the Shôkin-tei Teahouse of the Katsura Palace
(See explanation for previous plate.)

PLATE 100 ARCHITECTURE
EDO PERIOD [1615—1867]

ROOM FOR THE TEA CEREMONY IN THE SHÔKIN-TEI TEAHOUSE
(See explanation for Plate 98.)

INDEX

(Note: Figures in italics refer to numbered plates and captions; all other figures refer to page numbers.)

abbreviated technique; see gempitsu
Acalanatha; see Fudô Myô-ô
"Actor Bandô Mitsugorô, The," 43, *40*
Ajanta, 11
Amida, 20, 21, 27, *1, 43, 90*; images of, 21, 23, *51, 59*
"Amida and Two Attendants," 10, *51*
Amidism; see Amida; Pure Land sect
Amitabha; see Amida
Amoghapasa; see Fukû Kensaku Kannon
"Ancient Dance," 38
Andô Hiroshige; see Hiroshige
animal caricatures, 25, 28, *10, 11, 14*
Aoki Mokubei, 41, *36*
architecture, Asuka period, *85, 86*; Edo period, 40, *98–100*; Heian period, 17, 18, 20–21, *90, 91*; Kamakura period, 29–30, *92, 93*; Momoyama period, 36–37, *97*; Muromachi period, 34, 35, *94–96*; Nara period, 10, 11, 12–13, 18, *87–89*; Prehistoric period, 4, 5, *84*; residential, 22, 34, 37; and tea ceremony, 35
Asanga; see Muchaku
Asano Collection, *14*
Ashikaga, family, 27, 31, 34; Takauji, 31; Yoshimasa, 34; Yoshimitsu, 31, 34
Ashiya (type of kettle), 35, *82*
Asiatic influences, 3, 5, 14, *3*; see also Chinese, Indian, Korean
Asuka period, 6–9; architecture, *85–86*; ceramics, 9; metalwork, 9; painting, 8; sculpture, 6–8, 10, *45–48*; textiles, 8–9, *74*
atsuita (costume), *77*
"Autumn and Winter Landscapes," *21*
Avalokitesvara; see Kannon
Azuchi, 36–37

Basu Sennin, image of, 30, *63*
batik, 15, 16, 26
"bay," defined, 12
"Beauty," *42*
bell-like objects; see dôtaku
Bhaisajya-guru; see Yakushi Nyorai
Bishamon-ten, *9*
Bodhisattva, 14, 19–20, *1, 6, 17, 46, 49*
Brahma, *53*
brocade, 8–9, 16, *75*; Kantô, 8–9, *74*
"brocade pictures"; see nishiki-e
bronze, sculpture, 6, 10, *45, 49–51*;

metalwork, 4, 9, *83*
Buddha, at Nara, see Tôdaiji; of sun and moon, 13, *53, 55*
"Buddha Head," 10, *50*
Buddhism, 6–7, 10, 11–12, 16–17, 19, 20, 23, 27, 34, *58*; see also Pure Land; Shingon; Tendai; Zen
Buddhist, architecture, 6–7, 10–11, 12–13, 34, *85–96*; painting, 6, 19, 24, 27–28, *1, 3–6, 8–9, 12, 17*; sculpture, 6, 13, 20, 33–34, *45–57, 59–61, 63*
Buson; see Yosa Buson
Byôdô-in, Phoenix Hall, 21, 22, 23, *36, 59*

Candraprabhasa; see Gakkô Butsu
carving techniques, 20, 23
castle architecture, 36–37, 40, *97*
cave dwellings, 5
"Celebration under the Cherry Blossoms," 42, *26*
ceramics; see pottery; porcelain
Cézanne, 43
Ch'ang-an, 11
Chien-chên; see Ganjin
Chinese influence, 3, 5, 7, 9–10, 23, 29, 31, 41, 45, *1, 3, 50, 71*
Chinese-style, architecture, 10, 29, 34, *85–86, 93–95*; ceramics, 15, 31, 35, *65*; lacquer ware, *80*; painting, 11, 14, 15, 20, 24, 31–32, 33, 37, *21, 25, 28*; sculpture, 7–8, 10, 13, 30, *45, 46, 52*
Ch'ing, 41, 44
Chishô Daishi, *4*
Chô Densu; see Minchô
Chôgen, 29
Chôgo Sonshi-ji, *9*
Chôjirô, 67
Chou Mao-shu, *23*
"Chou Mao-shu Viewing the Lotus Flowers," 33, *23*
Chronicles of Japan; see Nihon Shoki
Chûgû-ji, 8, *48*
cinnabar, 13, *55, 62*
Cintamani; see Nyoirin Kannon
clay sculpture, 3, 4–5, 13, *44, 53–55, 61, 84*
clothing; see costume
Commission for the Protection of Cultural Properties, 15, *36, 79*
Confucianism, 10, 41
"Convenience of Farming," 41, *35*
"Cool Evening, A," 43
costume, 25–26, 30–31, 35, 44–45, *76, 77*; see also textiles

Daikan-daiji, 10
Degas, 43
Dengyô Daishi, 17
densu, 32
Deva Kings, Four, 13, *55*
Diamond Mandala, 18
Dôkyô, 16
domestic architecture; see architecture, residential
Donchô, *1*
Donyû, 67
door panels, painting on; see panel paintings
doors, sliding, 34
dôtaku, 5–6
"double hall"; see sôdô
dry-lacquer; see lacquer ware

e-Oribe; see "Picture Oribe"
Eastern Pagoda, 10, *87*
Edo period, 39–45; architecture, 40, *98–100*; lacquer ware, 45, *81*; painting, 40–42, *29–37, 42*; porcelain, 43–44, *69–73*; pottery, 43–44, *68*; textiles, 44–45, *77, 78*; woodblock prints, 42–43, *25, 38–41, 43*
Eitoku; see Kanô Eitoku
embroidery, 8, 16, 26, 31, 38, *76*
Engaku-ji, 29, *93*
"Enlightened Kings"; see Myô-ô
Enryaku-ji, 17, 18
"esoteric" Buddhism, 17, 18, 19, 20; see also Shingon; Tendai

feathers, used in painting, 14, *2*
"Fickle Type, The," 43, *39*
"Fifty-three Stages of the Tôkaidô, The"; see "Tôkaidô, The Fifty-three Stages of the"
"floating world," 42
fortress; see castle
"Four Accomplishments, The," 40, *27, 32*
Four Deva Kings; see Deva Kings, Four
"Frolic of the Animals," 25, 28, *10, 11, 14*
Fudô Myô-ô, 19, *4*
Fugen, Bodhisattva, 19–20, *6, 17*
"Fuji, Mt., Thirty-six Views of," 43, *41*
"Fuji, The Red"; see "Red Fuji, The"
"Fuji in a Storm," 41
"Fuji-san," 67
Fujiwara, family, 17, 20, 27; Michinaga, 21; Mitsunaga, *13*; Mitsuyoshi, *16*; Nobuzane, *18*; Taka-

nobu, 29, *16*; Takayoshi, **7**; Yorimichi, 21
fukinuke yatai, 24, 25
Fukû Kensaku Kannon, 13, *52–54*
Furuta Oribe Masashige, 38

Gakkô Butsu, *53, 55, 61*
Gaku-ô Zôkyû, 32
Ganjin, 13–14, *56, 88*
ʃardens, 22, 34, *96, 98*
gempitsu technique, *29*
Genji; *see Tale of Genji*
Ginkaku-ji, 34, *95*
glaze, 6, 15, 35, 38, 43, *65, 68, 69, 71–73*
"Golden Hall," Hôryû-ji, *1*
Golden Pavilion; *see* Kinkaku-ji
government and politics, 9–10, 16–17, 23, 26, 27, 31, 36, 39, 40, 41, 45
grave mounds; *see* tumuli
Great Buddha of Nara; *see* Tôdaiji
Greek sculpture, 7
"guardian deities, twelve," 19
Gupta art, 10
Gyokudô; *see* Uragami Gyokudô

"*Haboku* Landscape," 32, *22*
haboku technique, 32, 34, *22, 30*
Hachiman Shrine, *58*
Han-shan, 32, *19*
"Handbook on Hells," 28
"Handbook on Illnesses," *12*
haniwa, 4–5, 44, *84*
"*Haniwa* Head of a Girl," *44*
Hara, Kunizô, Collection of, *26*
Hara Collection, *5*
Harunobu, 43, *38*
Hasegawa Tôhaku, 37, *28*
Hashimoto Gahô, 41
Heian period, 16–27; architecture, 17, 18, 20–22, *90, 91*; lacquer ware, 26, *79*; painting, 19–20, *4–8*; pottery, 25; scroll painting, 24, *9–11*; sculpture, 19, 20, 22–23, *57–60*; textiles, 26
hemp, as lacquer base, 56; painting on, 14, *3*
hibutsu; *see* "secret Buddhas"
Hideyoshi; *see* Toyotomi Hideyoshi
Hiei, Mt., 17
Himeji Castle, 36–37, *97*
Hinduism, 13, 19
Hiroshige, 43, *43*
Hishikawa Moronobu; *see* Moronobu
history; *see* government and politics
"History of Mt. Shigi"; *see* "Shigi, Mt., History of"
Hô-ô-dô; *see* Byôdô-in, Phoenix Hall
Hôitsu; *see* Sakai Hôitsu
Hôjô, 27
Hôjô-ji, 21, 22
Hokke-dô; *see* Tôdaiji
Hokkyô, 22
Hokusai, 43, *41, 42, 43*
Hon'ami Kôetsu, 38, 41, *30, 67, 81*
honchi suijaku, 22
Hônen, 20

Hôryû-ji, 7, 8–9, 10, 13, *1, 45–48, 51, 74, 80, 85–87, 89*; *see also* Chûgû-ji
hôshu, 3
Hsia Kuei, 31

Ieyasu; *see* Tokugawa Ieyasu
Iga ware, 38, *68*
Igarashi Dôho, 45
Ike no Taiga, 41, *35*
Imari ware, 43–44, *70*
"immortal-poet pictures"; *see kasen-e*
Indian influence, 11, 13, 16, 29, *1, 49, 52–53, 92*
"Indian style," 29
Indra, 53
ink paintings; *see* monochrome painting
"Irises," 41, *33*
"iron-wire" lines, 11
ironwork, 35, *82*
Ise, Tales of; *see Tales of Ise*
Ise Monogatari; *see Tales of Ise*
Ise Shrine, 4, 5, 22
Ishii Genzô, *40*
Ishiyama-dera, 18, *92*
Itsukushima Shrine, *8*
Izumo, 22

Japanese style, 27, 45; architecture, 29–30; painting, 24, 37, 38; sculpture, 23; *see also yamato-e*
Jingan-ji; *see* Jingo-ji
Jingo-ji, 20, 29, *16, 57*
Jôchô, 22, 23, *59*
Jôdo sect; *see* Pure Land sect
Jômon period, design, 3, 4, *64*; pottery, 3, *64;* sculpture, 3
Jôruri-ji, 14, *60*
Josetsu, 32, *20*
Jukô-in, 27

Ka-ô Ninga, 32, *19*
Kabuki, *40*
Kaidan-dô; *see* Tôdaiji
Kaihô Yûshô, 37
Kaizan-dô, *see* Tôshôdai-ji
kakemono, paintings in the form of, 37, *19–24, 29, 36, 42*
Kakiemon (potter), 43–44, *69*
Kakiemon ware, *69, 70*
Kakuyû, Archbishop, 25, *9–11*
Kamakura period, 27–31; architecture, 29–30, *92, 93*; painting, 27–28, *16, 17*; pottery, 31; scroll painting, 28, *12–15, 18*; sculpture, 30, *61–63*
"Kambara," 43, *43*
Kannon, 7, 8, 13, *46–49, 52–54*
Kanô, School, 37, 38, 40, 41, 42, *23, 26, 28, 32*; Eitoku, 33, 37, *25, 27*; Hideyori, 37, *25*; Hôgai, 41; Masanobu, 33, *23*; Mitsunobu, 37; Motonobu, 33, 37, *27*; Naganobu, 37, *26*; Naonobu, 41, *26*; Sanraku, 37; Sanetsu, 37; Takanobu, 37, *32*; Tan'yû, 40, 42, *32*
Kanshin-ji, 19, 34, *94*

kanshitsu; *see* lacquer ware, dry-lacquer technique
"Kantô Brocade," 8–9, *74*
kara-e, 24
kara-yô; *see* Chinese-style, architecture
karaori, 45, *77*
kasaya, 56
kasen-e, 18
kasuri, 9, *74*
Katsura Palace, 40, *98–100*
Katsushika Hokusai; *see* Hokusai
Kawabata, Yasunari, Collection of, *35*
Kenzan, *73*
kettles, 35, *82*
Kichijô-ten, 14, *3, 60*
kimono; *see* costume; textiles
Kinkaku-ji, 34, *95*
Kitagawa Utamaro; *see* Utamaro
Kiyomasa, 43
Kiyomitsu, 43
Kiyomori; *see* Taira no Kiyomori
Kiyonaga, 43, *39*
Kiyonobu, 43
Ko Ôgimi, *18*
Kôben, 30, *62*
Kôbô Daishi, 17, 29, *17*
Kôetsu; *see* Hon'ami Kôetsu
Kôfuku-ji, 10, *50, 61, 62*
Koguryö, 6
Kômoku-ten, 55
Kongôbu-ji, 17
Korea, 5, 6, 9, 15, 36, 38, 43
Korean influence, 3, 5, 6, 38, 43, *47*
Kôrin, 41, 42, 45, *33, 34, 73, 81*
Kôshô, 29
kosode, 38, *76*
Kôya, Mt., 17, 18, 19, *4*
Kôzan-ji, *10, 11*
Kudara, *47*
Kudara Kannon, 8, *47, 48*
Kujaku Myô-ô, 19, *5*
Kûkai; *see* Kôbô Daishi
Kuratsukuribe no Tasuna, 6, 7
Kuratsukuribe no Tori; *see* Tori
Kutani ware, 44, *71*

lacquer ware, dry-lacquer technique, 13–14, 15–16, *52, 56*; Edo period, 45, *33, 81*; Heian period, 26, *79*; Momoyama period, 38–39, *80*; Muromachi period, 35; Nara period, 13–14, 15–16; painting on, 10–11; Prehistoric period, 3–4
landscape art, 14, 32, 33, 43, *20–23, 25, 27, 36, 41, 43*
lanterns, *62*
Li Li-wêng, *35*
Liang K'ai, 31, 37, *29*
Lotus Sutra, 6, 8
Lung-mên, 45, *85*

Ma Yüan, 31
Mahamayuri; *see* Kujaku Myô-ô
Mahasri; *see* Kichijô-ten
Maitreya; *see* Miroku
maki-e, 16, *26*, **35**, **38**, **39**, *79, 81*

"Man Catching a Catfish with a Gourd," 32, *20*
mandala, 18, 19
Manet, 43
Manjusri; *see* Monju
"Maple-Viewers at Mt. Takao," 37, 42, *25*
Maruyama Ôkyo, 42
Maruyama-Shijô School, 42
Masanobu; *see* Kanô, Masanobu
Matsubara, Gakunan, Collection of, *44*
merchant class, rise of, 40
metalwork, Asuka period, 9; Kamakura period, 30; Muromachi period, 35, *82–83*; Nara period, 13, *51–52*; Prehistoric period, 4, 5
Minamoto, family, 27; Yoritomo, 27, *16, 18*
Minchô, 32
Ming, 31, 41
"Miotsukushi," 38, *30*
Miroku (Maitreya) 6, 8, *48*
mirrors, 5
Mitsui, Takaharu, Collection of, 38
Mitsunaga; *see* Fujiwara Mitsunaga
Mitsunobu; *see* Tosa Mitsunobu
Miyamoto Musashi, 37–38, *29*
Miyazaki Yûzensai; *see* Yûzensai
Mokuan, 31
Mokubei; *see* Aoki Mokubei
Momoyama period, 36–39; architecture, 36–37, *97*; lacquer ware, 38–39, *80*; painting, 37–39, *27, 28*; pottery, 38, *66, 67*; screen painting, *26*; textiles, 38
"Mongaku Shônin, Portrait of," *16*
Monju, Bodhisattva, *17*
monochrome painting, 14–15, 20, 28, 31–32, 33, 37, *2, 10, 11, 14, 19, 20, 21, 24, 27–29, 35*
Mononobe clan, 6
Moronobu, 42, *37, 70*
mother-of-pearl inlay, 16, 26, *79*
Motonobu; *see* Kanô Motonobu
Mu Ch'i, 31, 37, *28*
Muchaku, 30, *61*
murals, 11, *1, 27, 32*; *see also* panel painting
Murasaki Shikibu, 7
Murayama Collection, *17*
Muromachi period, 31–36; architecture, 34–35, *94–96*; ceramics, 35, 36; gardens, 34, *96*; lacquer ware, 35; metalwork, 35, 36, *82, 83*; painting, 31–33, *19–25*; pottery, 35; sculpture, 33–34; textiles, 35
Musashi; *see* Miyamoto Musashi
Myô-ô, 19, *4, 5*
Myô-ô-in, *4*
Myôhô-in, *63*
Myôren, 25, *9*

Nabeshima ware, 44
Nagao Museum, *19, 29, 76, 78*
Nageire-dô; *see* Sambutsu-ji

Nagoya Municipality, *32*
Nakamura, Tomijirô, Collection of, *23*
Nakatsu-hime, *58*
Nanga School, 41, 42, *36*
Nara period, 9–16, architecture, 10, 11, 12, 13, *87–89*; ceramics, 15, *65*; lacquer ware, 15–16; metalwork, 13, *51–52*; painting, 10–11, 14–15, *1–3, 80*; pottery, 15, *65*; sculpture, 7, 10, 12, 13, *49–56*; textiles, 15, 16, *75–76*
nembutsu, 21
neolithic age, 3
Nezu Museum, *33, 68*
Nihon Shoki, 6
Nikkô, deity, *53, 55, 61*; place, 40
nimbus, 9
Nin'ami Dôhachi, 44, *73*
Ninsei, 44, *72*
Nishijin, 45
nishiki-e, 38
Niten; *see* Miyamoto Musashi
Nobunaga; *see* Oda Nobunaga
Noh costume, *76, 77*
Nomura, Fumihide, Collection of, *24*
Nonomura Ninsei; *see* Ninsei
Northern Wei, 8
"Northern-Painting," 41
Nyoirin Kannon, *48*

Oda Nobunaga, 36, 37
Ogata Kenzan; *see* Kenzan
Ogata Kôrin; *see* Kôrin
Ogawa Haritsu, 45
Okada, Mokichi, Collection of, *31*
Ôkyo; *see* Maruyama Ôkyo
Oribe ware, 38, *66*
Owari, 25, 31

pagoda, 10, 12, 17, 18, *86, 87, 92*
painting, Asuka period, 8; Edo period, 40–42, *29–37, 42*; Heian period, 19–20, *4–8*; Kamakura period, 27–28, *12–18*; Momoyama period, 37–39, *26–28*; Muromachi period, 31–33, *19–25*; Nara period, 10–11, 14–15, *1–3, 80*; *see also* screen painting; scroll painting
paleolithic age, 3
panel painting, 24, 37, *27*; *see also* murals
papier-mâché, *56*
Pekché, 6, *47*
Phoenix Hall; *see* Byôdô-in
"Picture Oribe," 66
"piles of rings"; *see wazumi*
Pillow Book, of Sei Shônagon, 28, *14*
"Pine Trees," *28*
pit houses, 5
"Plum Tree," *27*
Po-hai, 15
poets, portraits of, *18*
politics; *see* government and politics
Polynesia, 3, 9, *74*
porcelain, Edo period, 43–44, *69–73*;

Kamakura period, 31; Momoyama period, 38; Nara period, 15; *see also* pottery
portraiture, 7, 13–14, 27, 29, *2, 16–20, 23, 40, 61, 63*
potter's wheel, 3, 4, 6, 35
pottery, Asuka period, 9; Edo period, 43–44, *68*; Heian period, 25; Kamakura period, 31; Momoyama period, 38, *66, 67*; Muromachi period, 35; Nara period, 15, *65*; Prehistoric period, 3–4, 6, *64*; *see also* porcelain
Prehistoric period, 3–6; architecture, 4, 5, *84*; lacquer ware, 3–4; metalwork, 4–5; pottery, 3–4, 6, *64*; sculpture, 3, 4–5, *44*
"Priest Ganjin, The," 13, *56*
printed textiles, 16
Pure Land sect, 20–21, 23, 27

ra, 16
Rai Sanyô, *36*
raku ware, 38, *67*
"Red Fudô of Mt. Kôya," 19, *4*
"Red Fuji, The," *41*
"reduced-stroke" technique; *see gem-pitsu*
Reimei-kai, *7*
religion; *see* Buddhism; Confucianism; Hinduism; Shinto
residential architecture; *see* architecture, residential
Rôben, 13
"rope design"; *see* Jômon pottery
Ryôan-ji garden, 34, *96*

Saichô; *see* Dengyô Daishi
Sakai Collection, *13*
Sakai Hôitsu, 41, *34*
Sakai, Tadamasa, Collection of, *67*
Sakaida Kakiemon; *see* Kakiemon
Sakyamuni, 7, 18, 20, *45, 46*; *see also* Buddha; "Shaka Nyorai"
"Sakyamuni Triad," 7, *45, 46, 48, 51*
Samantabhadra; *see* Fugen Bodhisattva
Sambutsu-ji, Nageire-dô, 18, *91*
sandalwood, 19, 20
Sanjûsangen-dô; *see* Myôhô-in
Sano kettle, 35
screen painting, 14, 15, 24, 37, 38, 39, 41, *2, 25, 26, 30, 31, 33, 34*
scroll painting, 8, 24, 28, 33, *8, 9–11, 12–15, 18*
sculpture, Asuka period, 6–8, 10, *45–48*; Heian period, 19, 20, 22–23, *57–60*; Kamakura period, 30, *61–63*; Muromachi period, 33–34; Nara period, 7, 10, 11, 12, 13, *49–56*; Prehistoric period, 3, 4–5, *44*
seasons, the four, as subject of art, 25
"secret Buddhas," *46, 54*
Sei Shônagon, *14*; *see also Pillow Book*

Seika-dô Foundation, 30, 72
Sekido Collection, 12
Sesshû, 32, 21, 22, 24, 28
Sesshû V; see Hasegawa Tôhaku
Sesson, 33, 24
Seto ware, 25, 31, 35, 38
"Shaka Nyorai," 45
Sharaku, 43, 40
Shi-Tennô-ji, 7, 86
Shiba Tachito, 7
"Shigi, Mt., History of," 25, 28, 9, 13, 15
Shih-tê, 19
Shijô School, 41, 42
shinden architecture, 22, 34, 90, 95, 98
Shingon sect, 17, 18, 92, 94
Shinto, 20, 22, 28, 58
"Shô Kannon," 13, 49
shoin architecture, 34, 37
Shôkin-tei Teahouse; see Katsura Palace
Shôkoku-ji, 32
Shôsô-in, 14–15, 2, 65, 74, 75
Shôtoku, Prince, 6–7, 9, 10
"Shrike on a Dead Branch," 37, 29
Shrine of Lady Tachibana; see Tachibana, Lady
Shûbun, 32, 33
Shugaku-in, 40
Shûkongô-jin, 13, 54
Silla, 6
Silver Pavilion; see Ginkaku-ji
Siva, 13
"Sketches from Nature," 42
Sôami, 96
sôdô, 18, 22
Soga clan, 6
Sôtatsu, 38, 41, 42, 30, 33, 34, 73, 81
Sôtatsu-Kôrin School, 42
South Sea Islands; see Polynesia
"Southern-Painting" style; see Nanga School
stencil dyeing, 15, 16, 26
"Storm at Sea," 33, 24
"Story of the Latter Three Years' Campaign," 28, 15
"Story of Tomo no Dainagon," 28, 13
stupas, 92
sumi-e; see monochrome painting
"Summer and Autumn Plants," 41, 34
Sun Goddess, 16
Sung, 7, 15, 29, 30, 31, 33, 37, 21, 23
"Sunny Morning at Uji," 36
sutras, 24, 25, 6, 8
Suzuki Harunobu; see Harunobu
swords; see weapons

Tachibana, Lady, Shrine of, 10, 51
Taiga; see Ike no Taiga
Taika Reform, 9, 10
Taira, family, 27, 8; no Kiyomori, 27, 8; no Shigemori, 21, 16
Taizô-in, 20

Takanobu; see Fujiwara Takanobu
Takayoshi; see Fujiwara Takayoshi
Tale of Genji, The, 24, 25, 28, 7, 9, 13, 14, 30, 98
Tales from Uji, 13
Tales of Ise, 33, 81
Tamamushi Shrine, 8, 80
T'ang, 9, 10, 11, 13, 15, 23
Tani Bunchô, 41
Tankei, 30, 63
Tanomura Chikuden, 41, 36
Tan'yû; see Kanô Tan'yû
tapestry, 8
tarashikomi technique, 30
tatami, 34
Tawaraya Sôtatsu; see Sôtatsu
tea-ceremony, 34–35, 36; architecture, 35, 40, 99, 100; gardens, 98; utensils, 35, 38, 44, 67, 68, 72, 82
"Ten Conveniences," 35
"Ten Joys," 35
"Ten Physiognomical Studies of Women," 39
Tendai sect, 17, 4, 6
tenjiku-yô; see "Indian style"
"Tentô-ki," 30, 62
textiles, Asuka period, 8–9, 74; Edo period, 44–45, 77–78; Heian period, 25, 26; Kamakura period, 30–31; Momoyama period, 38; Muromachi period, 35; Nara period, 15, 16, 75–76
"Thirty-six Immortal Poets, The," 18
"Thirty-six Views of Mt. Fuji"; see "Fuji, Mt."
"Thousand-Armed Kannon, Twenty-eight Attendants of," 63
tie-dyeing, 15, 16, 31
T'ien-lung-shan, 45
"Tiger," 40
Toba, Bishop of; see Kakuyû
Tôdaiji and the Great Buddha of Nara, 12–13, 14, 29, 30, 2, 9, 52–55, 61
Tôhaku; see Hasegawa Tôhaku
Tôin-dô; see Yakushi-ji
"Tôkaidô, The Fifty-three Stages of the," 43
tokonoma, 34
Tokugawa, family, 39, 41; Ieyasu, 36, 39, 40
Tokugawa, Muneyoshi, Collection of, 34
Tokyo National Museum, 6, 12, 21, 22, 25, 28, 37, 40, 41, 43, 64, 65, 70, 71, 74, 75, 77, 81, 82, 84
"Tomo no Dainagon, The Story of," 28, 13
Tori, 7, 8, 45–47
torii, 22
Torii family; see Kiyomasa; Kiyomitsu; Kiyonaga; Kiyonobu
Tosa, School, 33, 38, 41; Mitsunobu, 33; Mitsuyoshi, 38
Tôshô-gû, 40
Tôshôdai-ji, 12, 13, 56, 88
Tôshûsai Sharaku; see Sharaku

Toyotomi Hideyoshi, 36, 37, 38, 39, 43
tsukuri-e, painting style, 7, 13
tumuli, 4, 6
Tung Yüan, 31

Uji Shûi Monogatari; see Tales from Uji
ukiyo-e, 42; see also woodblock prints
Unkei, 30, 61–63
Uragami Gyokudô, 41
Utamaro, 43, 39

Vaisravana; see Bishamon-ten
Vajrapani; see Shûkongô-jin
Van Gogh, 43
Vasu; see Basu Sennin

wa-yô; see Japanese style, architecture
wabi, 35, 36
wall painting; see murals
Watanabe, Kazan, 41
wax, 16, 45
wazumi, 4
weapons, 4, 5, 30
Western influence, 39, 31
"Westerners Playing Music," 39, 31
"wet drapery," 10
wheel design, 79
"Winter Landscape," 32, 21
"Woman," 37
"Woman on a Veranda," 43, 38
"Women of Ten Physiognomical Types," 39
woodblock prints, 42–43, 25, 37–41, 43

Yakushi-ji, 10, 13, 14, 3, 49, 58, 87
Yakushi Nyorai, 20, 57
Yamato, 4, 44
Yamato Bunka-kan, 18
yamato-e, 24, 25, 29, 33, 37, 38, 41, 7, 8, 14, 25, 30; see also Japanese style, painting
Yayoi culture, 4
Yayoi pottery, 4, 6, 64
Yohô-in, 83
Yoritomo; see Minamoto no Yoritomo
Yosa Buson, 41, 35
Yoshihara, Moshichi, Collection of, 42
Yoshimitsu; see Ashikaga Yoshimitsu
Yoshino, Tomio, Collection of, 80
Yüan, 31, 33
Yume-dono; see Hôryû-ji
Yume-dono Kannon, 7, 8, 9, 46
Yün-kang, 45, 85
Yûshô; see Kaihô Yûshô
Yûzen dyeing, 45, 78
Yûzensai, 78

Zen Buddhism, 29, 31, 32, 33–34, 36, 19, 20, 23, 24, 93, 95, 96, 98
zenki, 20

T

DATE DUE